D1457397

Judith Stoutland

the gayety of grace

the gayety of grace

edna hong

*grace!*

*Edna Hong*

augsburg
publishing house
minneapolis
minnesota

# contents

*But the bare goodness* of God is what ought rather to be preached and known above all else, and we ought to learn that even as God saves us out of pure goodness, without any merit or works, so we in turn should do the works without reward or self-seeking for the sake of the bare goodness of God.

MARTIN LUTHER

*The ancient Christian* images of "heaven" and "hell" have taken on a new significance in our own age. Hell is anywhere on earth where people think their life has to be earned, where people try to realize themselves in their own achievements and successes, where in consequence people achieve and constantly have to make new achievements, where they put a fence around what is their own, grudging life to others and disputing with them the living space which they have in common. But heaven is everywhere on earth where people receive life as a gift, where they thankfully receive their own existence and everything that belongs to it, when they live with open hearts, and where as a consequence they are open to others and give them with all their hearts what they themselves have only received as a gift.

HEINZ ZAHRNT

*Everything is a grace . . .* everything is the direct effect of our Father's love—difficulties, contradictions, humiliations, all the soul's miseries, her burdens, her needs – everything, because through them, she learns humility, realizes her weakness. Everything is a grace because everything is God's gift. Whatever be the character of life or its unexpected events – to the heart that loves, all is well.

ST. THERESE

the gayety of grace

the curtain raiser

To be honest, this is a preface, but it is not called a preface because most people pay little or no attention to prefaces, forewords, and preludes, just as they pass vacantly through narrow hallways to houses, through skinny vestibules to the cars of a passenger train, or through the meager mouths that usher them into the great stomachs of jet planes. But this preface is too important for negligence of that sort. The reader who chooses to skip the preface may never see the curtain of comprehension rise upon this play. If play it be!

Six of my several selves (Who, may I ask, speaks from a pure self?) recently played out this drama in my head and went on their way singing their song of Grace. But I came back to fit it all together to pass it on to you – and from you hopefully to another. And if it passes from you to another, then perhaps it is truly a play, and this may prove to be the best way, the very best of ways, to re-enact a play!

This play, *The Gayety of Grace,* takes place in the theater of all our torments and delights, the top of the human house, that two percent of our adult body which distinguishes one individual from another far more than the color of the hair and the shape of the nose, that one-fiftieth of us which makes life on earth a heaven or hell or, perhaps more correctly, something that stumbles and flounders between the two. All eight acts are played out in that neatly fitted, boxed-in-bone brain which on the slightest stimulus creates the widest effects and side-effects.

An architectural blueprint of the stage would call for an arched and frescoed vault, for that is what the human skull is when divested of all its visceral stuff – the stuff of life! The sets and props? Forget them, for a genius of a director could not authentically represent or even suggest that nutshell which can contain the continent of Africa one instant, the whole world the next, and the universe the next. Since it is utterly impossible to represent the swift and constant change of mental scenery or to depict the gentle heaving of the brain with every breath we take, simply think of a Great Hall, a pleasant space and not at all formidable. Since dialog is going on there constantly, it is called Dialectical Hall.

The two cerebral hemispheres attached to one brain stem in one skull is, of course, *my* skull, *my* brain, *my* mind. In other words, I am guilty of that most shocking indiscretion – the laying bare of the mind, a far more intimate exposure than physical nudity or laying bare the heart. Some more affluent minds may think the locale of the play a modest, even shabby, place, but it is hoped that they nevertheless will find it attractively shabby and modest. Only those who go to bed every night clutching their own immovable mind-sets and dear familiar mind-scapes and get up every morning still clenching the same will find my brain threatening. But let them not panic too soon, for what may look like a horrendous and frightening new philosophy may not be a new philosophy at all, but a very old philosophy, a philosophy so old that it looks new. Furthermore, it may not be philosophy at all, but theology. It may even be Christian theology!

## the characters

1. ME-R is my Respectable, Establishment self. She is a realist, very rational, somewhat reactionary, reliable, and responsible. Because she is religious, she is not entirely unreceptive to the new but finds it difficult to welcome new ideas and thoughts into the home of the mind, especially if they are uninvited and unexpected guests. Often she cannot conceal facial expressions that speak: "Where on earth did *you* come from!" In some ways she is much like Mrs. Darling in *Peter Pan,* always tidying up my mind, picking up scraps and rags of thoughts and putting them into properly labelled drawers.

2. ME-I is everything that starts with *imp*—impulsive, impertinent, impudent, impetuous, improvident – and often impenitent. She has been a rebel ever since first grade in a rural Wisconsin school, when she defied her mother

(who would not let her go barefoot until May 30) and her teacher (who would not let children go barefoot who came from home in shoes) by taking off her shoes and stockings on the way to school, hiding them under a bridge, and arriving at school unshod and home again shod.

3. ME-T does not know if she is a Philosopher or a Theologian but actually is neither. Any third- or fourth-rate philosopher or theologian could back her quickly into a corner, from which she would calmly and without any embarrassment extricate herself by appealing to the Philosopher Partner of the Corporate Self to please explain "what I am thinking." Which he would do – and most patiently. Me-T may be called a Theologian only because of her hound-dog passion for chasing meanings out of their common homely holes in plain everyday life to a place where she can look at them with her theologically untrained eyes and get a new perspective on them.

4. ME-N is an amateur Naturalist and ardent Nature-lover and is *anti*-but-not-necessarily-*un*-intellectual. She gardens – mostly flowers – and her fingernails are usually black. Or bread-dough-encrusted, for she makes bread from home-ground wheat and honey. Her usual attire is blue jeans or something resembling a shapeless burlap bag the color of a horsechestnut.

5. ME-E is an Ecstatic. She dances in solitude to Bach and Vivaldi and in public often seems to be looking at Burning Bushes. She experiences a strange rapture every time she recites the Nicene Creed or hears monks intoning the Gregorian chants. She reads poetry, of course, and tries to write it but has no grandiose illusions about herself as a poet. She shuns crowds, seeks solitude, and is positively (as against negatively) unclubbable.

6. ME-D is my Despair, despair so anguished she cannot weep and does not often speak. The other Me's are made unhappy by small misfortunes. Despair knows the anguish of the Great Misfortune, the human predicament. She knows what is and knows what ought to be, and the disparity and distance between the two is her dejection.

7. I, the Corporate ME, is not necessarily the healthy, integrated myself who marches onstage alone, all her several selves joined together and speaking as one! She may, in fact, be a mask for one or all of the others, a protective front when one or all of them feels threatened.

Oddly enough, *The Gayety of Grace,* a play in eight acts, is not precipitated by Me-T the Theologian, but by Me-E, the Ecstatic. Being a solitary and sequestered self, Me-E does not often communicate her concerns to the public, not even to her other selves. For Me-E to miss the joy in life is to miss all. It troubles her to see that for most people "life falls dead like dough instead of soaring away like a balloon into the colors of the sunset," (lines she was surprised to find in Robert Louis Stevenson one day). Where does joy reside? Thanks to her religious upbringing, she associates joy with the Grace of God, but she feels no thanks to her religious upbringing for the preacher-teacher-taught understanding that the Grace of God is a state of being pleasing to God and is entirely at his discretion. She cannot stomach such a capricious God! Therefore when Me-E overheard a pious, upright neighbor apply that most vapid of hackneyed phrases, "There but for the Grace of God go I," to another neighbor who is an alcoholic, she flew into a private rage and searched the *Oxford Book of Quotations* to find who had said that first. She found it attributed to John Bradford (1510-1555), who on seeing some "criminals" being led away to the gallows is supposed to have said, "But for the Grace of God there goes John Bradford." Just a few pages distant from John Bradford's immortal words, she found the silly, irreverent ditty British soldiers bellowed with brazen bravado in the trenches of World War I:

O Death, where is thy sting – a– ling – ling,
O grave, thy vict – or – ee – ee – ee?
The bells of hell go ting – a – ling – ling
for you but not for me – e – e – e!

Upon reading that, Me-E exclaimed: "Oh, John Bradford, you sound so humble, so pious and edifying, so impeccably, so unimpeachably Christian! But you could just as well have recited that silly ditty!"

Being Me-E, my Ecstatic self who puts her mental mullings into poems, she wrote some of her reactions to John Bradford's "Grace" down on paper, but before she could hide it away under lock and key with her other poems, Me-N, my nature-loving self, called her to come hear a catbird singing its marvelous repertoire. In short, Me-E forgot her poem; Me-R, my neat respectable self, picked it up in her persistent housecleaning; and the whole household of selves was plunged into this sometimes discordant and violent drama.

discord in the house

act I

*The house at the top of the body is unusually quiet and one gathers that the*
*mind is drifting and idling in a state of floating thinking. No tenants are to*
*be seen in Dialectical Hall save for Me-R at her everlasting self-appointed task*
*of picking up the rags and tags of thoughts and putting them into their proper*
*drawer. Poor dear, she even has a drawer for thoughts too trivial to save!*
*She finds the* Oxford Dictionary of Quotations *on the floor where Me-Ecstasy*
*left it and, being like some librarians who feel that books should be in place*
*on the shelf and not out being read, she moves off in the direction of the*
*library. Noticing the loose papers in the book, she takes them out and reads*

23

*what Me-E wrote in response to the quotation on Grace attributed to John Bradford and the silly ditty about the bells of hell. As she reads her face takes on a look that says far more than "Where on earth did you come from?" In fact, it shrieks, "From what littered limbo of sloppy thinking did this come!!"*

ME-R (*loudly*): Who's responsible for this drivel about Grace! (*All the other Me's emerge from their cells and cluster around her.*) It's obscene, I tell you!

ME-T: You *must* mean incorrect. How could anyone write anything improper or indecent about Grace!

ME-R: Obscene! Gay Grace – it's obscene!

ALL THE ME'S: Read it! Let's hear it!

ME-R: Not on your life! It's going in the garbage can where trash like this belongs. (*Me-T demurs and quietly takes it from her, scans it quickly, and then reads aloud.*)

Black humor is the perennial game
soldiers play in men's perennial wars.

Gray grace is the game grace-proud men
play in the shadow of the cross.

Gray grace is the game grace-proud,
finger-pointing men play inside
God's very own game—Grace.

It's a dull game – gray grace –
mirthless and measured,

played with accepted, conventional rules,
utterly predictable
utterly reliable
no surprises
no risks
no sudden laughter,
and grace is on their side, of course!
Gray congealed grace, that is,
which is no grace at all –
certainly not God's gay Grace!

Gay Grace is a happiness so great that it dances.

> So David went and brought up the ark of the Lord
> from the house of Obededom to the city of David
> with rejoicing. . . . And David danced before the
> Lord with all his might and David was girded with
> a linen ephod.

Gray grace is a discontent so great that it kills joy.

> And as the ark of the Lord came into the city of
> David, Michal the daughter of Saul looked out of
> the window, and saw King David leaping and
> dancing before the Lord, and she despised him in
> her heart.

Gay Grace is a happiness so great that it feels
blessed – and can bless!

> And when David had finished offering the burnt
> offerings and the peace offering he blessed the
> people in the name of the Lord . . . . and David
> returned to bless his household.

Gray grace is discontent so great that it sulks
in the sun of Grace and curses the brightness.

> But Michal the daughter of Saul came out to meet
> David, and said, "How the King of Israel honored
> himself today, uncovering himself today before the
> eyes of his servants' maids, as one of the vulgar
> fellows shamelessly uncovers himself!"

And David, still in the ecstasy of Grace, said to
his wife Michal in her ecstasy of rage

> "It is before the Lord I dance . . . and I will make
> merry before the Lord."

Dance, dance,
dance, man dance,
dance to the Lord
dance to the Lord of the Dance!

Laugh, laugh,
laugh, woman, laugh
laugh the terrestial
laugh the celestial
laugh the unquenchable
laugh of grace!

ME-R: Dancing, laughing! It's dangerous, I tell you, it's dangerous! *(Me-T wrinkles her brow and scans the poem again.)*

ME-T: *Remissio peccatorum sol dich frölich machen. Hoc est caput doctrinae, Christianae, et tamen periculosissima praedication.*

ME-N *(who dislikes intellectual pretensions as much as she dislikes plastic plants)*: Oh quit trying to impress us. If you can't talk our language, shut up!

ME-T *(unruffled, for she actually was not trying to impress anybody but was just making another of her exciting "piecing together" discoveries)*: It's a quotation from Luther's *Table Talk,* which is why it's such a queer mixture of German and Latin. "Forgiveness of sins ought to make you rejoice; this is the very heart of Christianity, and yet it is a mighty dangerous thing to preach."

ME-R: "A mighty dangerous thing to preach!" Hear, hear! Luther said it. It must be right!

ME-IMP: Hear, hear! Luther said it, and of course he's always right! "Forgiveness of sins ought to make you rejoice. This is the very heart of Christianity." So . . .

Laugh, laugh,
laugh, woman, laugh

laugh the terrestial
laugh the celestial
laugh the unquenchable
laugh of Grace!


ME-R *(with an Establishment sneer)*: Aha, so it was *you* who wrote it! I might have known! You seem to have a bad case of the uplifts. Or is it chronic religious sentimentality? Or maybe acute spiritual diarrhea? There is a strong odor of flatus in the room. You had better take your "It's a glad, glad world" thoughts and go to bed.

ME-I *(sassily)*: If there is any gas present, Madame Respectable, it is laughing gas. As for my health, I never felt better.

ME-T *(who has lost the connection again, as she always does when she forgets to knot the thread)*: But your theology, dear! You do seem to have been coaxed into the New Theology of Holy Hilarity. Every day a Red Letter Day. Every act a holy act. Relax in the Lord! Hallelujah! Go to bed in the Lord. Get up in the Lord. Relieve yourself in the Lord. Hallelujah! Strum the guitars, shake the castanets, clap your hands, stamp your feet. Hallelujah! Shout to the Lord with a glad, glad voice! *(Me-T stops abruptly, obviously flustered.)* Excuse me, I was carried away.

ME-I: Indeed you were! Backward! You almost backed up 4000 years and banished a poet named David along with the New Theology!

ME-R: It isn't theology at all. Your gay Grace is pink politics! You have always chased after the Pied Pipers of Paradise Now! *(At this all the reactionary thoughtlings clustering around Me-R begin to chant: "Me-I is a commie! Me-I is a commie!")*

ME-ECSTASY *(blazes with anger, pushes the reactionary thoughtlings aside, and*

28

*stands before Me-R but includes Me-T in her fusillade)*: Stop it! Leave Me-I alone! She didn't write that about gay Grace. It was I. Do you want to know why? The concept of Grace we live by is – why, it's like an angleworm's view of the world! "Saved by Grace," we say—and we mean saved for immortality. But we are saved for *life* first. God's Grace resurrects the dead here and now, in life, for life! God's Grace resurrects the poet that died young in the solid and the stolid. God's Grace resurrects the dead sensibility to wonder and rapture. God's Grace resurrects the dead and buried life inside of us that makes life outside of us a long and empty yawn.

ME-T: Take care, Ecstasy, take care! *(She falls on her knees in mock supplication.)* Oh, Christ Jesus, heighten my consciousness, strengthen my will, intensify my perceptions, make me radiant, make me vivid, make me glad, make me gay! Oh, no, my dear, if all you want to do is remove mental cramps and strengthen the muscles of consciousness, then take drugs, join an encounter group, do yoga exercises – but don't for theology's sake prostitute the Christian faith! *(Whereupon all the thoughtlings clustering around Me-T begin to chant: "Me-E is a hippie! Me-E is a hippie! Me-E is a hippie!" Pandemonium breaks out in Dialectical Hall, and Me-Imp and Me-Nature-lover run around screaming and shouting.)*

ME-I and ME-N: You fools, you fools, you fools, you fools! She isn't a hippie, she isn't a hippie, she isn't a hippie at all! She means you don't have to be a hippie when you have Grace. You don't have to take drugs or do yoga when you have Grace. Grace is enough! Grace is chock-full. Grace is sufficient. Do you hear? Grace is sufficient! *(But nobody hears them for the noise, and Me-E, being an Ecstatic – they crash fast! – crumples in a heap and cries bitterly.)*

the
mysterious  visitor
act II

*Like a violent wave all my several wrangling selves and all their jangling squabbling thoughts and thoughtlings surge forward and back, forward and back, and when the hub of the hubbub is deep in Lower Hall, there crawls forth out of the furrow of the Fissure of Orlando and over a gray convoluted ridge into the Upper Hall a lithe and sinewy figure in bright red trunks and a sky-blue T-shirt. Like a child's parti-colored ball he rolls into the hall, uncoils, springs to his feet like a spring that is sprung. A clown? An acrobat? A juggler? A tumbler? A ballet dancer? A fool? Poised on toe tips for an endless instant he suddenly cuts the pull of earth with a flick of the feet. Like a startled bird he rises in the air, arches, and somersaults three times. Yes, by the shades of Nijinsky, he flips over three times before landing. All my Me's drift toward this flouter of gravity as in a dazzled dream and cannot believe their eyes.*

ME-N *(in deepest awe):* My God, what grace!

ME-I: Whee!

*(Suddenly, with a roguish twinkle, as if to show he is not just a limber, graceful tumbler, he scoops twelve brown and lustrous chestnuts from the floor and flings them in the air. To say he juggles them is hardly fair, he gives them wings. When his act is over he laughingly tosses two nuts to each of them and makes as if to go. But Me-Imp rushes up and touches his arm.)*

ME-I: Oh, Mr. Juggler, Mr. Tumbling Man, I don't know if you are sage or simpleton, but this I know: you levitate the most leaden weight. Oh, Sir, can you help us? Can you play games with our foolish and fixed ideas? Can you unjumble our muddled values? Can you tumble our man-made distinctions? Can you raise lowness into loftiness? Turn tears into laughter? Nothing into everything?

*(If he has words he does not speak them. It is Me-R who explodes the silence with harsh command.)*

ME-R: Be gone, you silly, guileless pagan fool. Or hanky-panking faking fiend. From time immemorial it has always been a time of danger when church-men turn to revelry. You cannot pepsinate the four-square Gospel. You cannot hallucinate or titillate the steadfast faithful. Our God is immutable. Our faith is unchangeable. Take your apocryphal gay Grace and go!

34

*(Obediently he turns to go, but Me-E springs before him and stares at him transfixed.)*

ME-E: Fool of God, you do not fool me! I know you by your *jestures!* Tell me, I must know—it is the most urgent question in my life. Is there a gravity so grievous that you cannot spin it into the sky-blue of Grace? And if you can, then why are we so grounded, so out of it, so out of the game of Grace?

*(Again he does not answer, and this time it is a new voice that shatters the stillness. It is Me-D, my Despair. Advancing toward him, her face is white as plants that grow in gloom, and her eyes burn like an animal's in the dark. Her cry shakes the jointless bones of the brain-house.)*

ME-D: I know a weight you cannot lift, a ten-ton millstone. Can you levitate the decomposed body of a raped ten-year-old girl? Can you dance with that weight of woe? Can you look at that thought and be glad-glad-glad?

*(The words "glad-glad-glad" echo from gray convoluted ridge to gray convoluted ridge, and the silence that follows is stunned. And there at their feet, foul and focal, concentrated in one long-searched-for but too-late-found small body of violated innocence lies the lifeless, inert enormity, the abominable thought of all the past and present and future foulness of all the evil done, being done, and about to be done to innocence. The odor of despair fills the Hall. The place is great with dread, and all my several selves move back. And he, the juggler and the tumbler? Swiftly he kneels and bends to kiss what once were lips. But he does not weep. Not then— not until he scans their several faces, not until his eyes pass from face to face and see the total darkness of their despair. Then he weeps, he weeps indeed, and everything becomes infinitely heavy. Everything except his light-limbed body, his graceful buoyant body. Three times he circles the de-*

*composing body and then bends swiftly down. Oh, it is not a tortuous, humble, sagging, knee-bending bow! It is a grand, majestic, princely bow, feet and knees vertical and true to a heavenward line. Head and heart graciously saluting all that is flat, fallen, and prostrate. Me-Despair leans toward him, not bitterness, but love and pity in her eyes.)*

ME-D: Oh, Sir, whoever you are—Sir Galahad or Don Quixote—once in Jotunheim, the ice giants' country, the great god Thor was asked to lift a cat, a great gray cat, and he could not. It was the Midgard serpent in disguise, the serpent that circles the earth and holds its tail in its mouth. Evil Loki's baleful, monster child. It is the power of Evil itself you are trying to lift. You cannot do it. It is impossible!

*(He smiles, that's all. He only smiles, and it is as if a wind clears the room of putrid death and dread and earth releases its clutching hold. Slowly he raises the grievous burden above his head, holds it lightly on open palms of outstretched arms. Slowly he turns that all might see, slowly but lightly his feet begin to move across the floor in solemn, stately dance. Reverently and without uttering a word my selves move slowly in grave and measured movement into a ceremonious circle. They dance with arms upraised, as if they, too, hold high that monstrous burden. They revolve around the juggler. It is Despair who whispers softly to the slow cadence of the dance.)*

ME-D: Dance, dance,
dance, Despair, dance.
Dance to the Lord,
dance to the Lord of the Dance!

a visit to

the sub-sub-basement

act III

*"How did he do it?" they ask each other the next morning when they awake—Me-R first, for sleep to her is time misspent; Me-D last, because sleep to her is a kind of suicide. "How did he do it? What really happened?" Some think it a dream, one of the happier apparitions that washes up on the shores of consciousness from the seas of the subconscious, and not the usual garbage of shattered, shipwrecked hopes and dreams.*

ME-N: But he was too vivid, too real!
ME-T: What is real? *(They all groan.)*

ME-D: Listen! *(They all do, for Despair seldom speaks.)* What we saw and experienced last night was the truth, the whole truth, and nothing but the truth. But he was a mime, and he mimed us a play. At first we thought it a vaudeville act—and then a tragedy—but he turned it into a magnificent comedy and turned us from spectators to actors – and finally to ballet dancers. Today we must spell out the truth for ourselves, for only the truth that is truth for us is truth.

ME-N: I have no time to spell out any truth that isn't easy, simple, ordinary truth, plain, honest, gospel truth. Besides, I'm going to walk in the woods today. Goodbye!

ME-T *(grabbing her arm):* You're always running away from meanings! Despair is right. Where shall we have our spelling class?

ME-D *(pointing down):* Down there.

ALL OF THEM *(appalled):* Down *there?*

ME-D: Yes, down there—the most unredeemed place in man! The sub-sub-basement of being, the subliminal self, the subconscious.
*(There is a sputtering of protests which Me-Ecstatic perhaps articulates best.)*

ME-E: I once wrote a poem which began like this:

Were I to see projected on a great screen
a chart of the world of my being
I would in loathing deny that it was I,
and believe my own denial.
Were I to glimpse with a gnat's eye view
the Spirit's eye view of my in-country
I would perish!

I don't believe, Despair, that any of us wants to see the geography of our innermost.

ME-R *(slowly and hesitantly):* None of us wants to go down there, but maybe we ought to. My special revelation last night was that I have a strong sense of duty to my God, but not a strong sense of joy in him. Maybe down there I'll find out what's wrong.

ME-I *(with more bravado than bravery):* O.K! O.K! Let's go! Let's go! Let's make the stink tank a think tank – just for today. Despair, lead the way. You know the place best. Where's the elevator? Press the down button.

ME-D *(laughing):* Oh, you are a silly! But I wish I were more like you than me. I don't know the place any better than you. I'm only haunted by it. *(Nevertheless Despair leads the way down many a stair, through many a door, and a very last door to an underground room that is not light and is not dark, is not big and not small, not lonely and not lively. In fact, it is a cool, subdued, and tranquil kind of place.)*

ME-D *(looking around in amazement):* I thought it would be a foul sewery sort of place with a sump pump dredging bilge water up into the consciousness!

ME-E *(equally amazed):* I thought it would be like a root cellar I found one day one May, where a ton of light-starved, winter-stored potatoes lay. They'd sprouted ghastly ghostly stems that mounted to the ceiling. They were lank and rank, a silent forest of doomed and dying shapes.

ME-R: I thought it would be full of crypts and closets, sealed up cells, and they again filled with bones and clandestine secrets, lusts and hates and all such odious things. This subterranean room looks more like a repository or depository, a kind of storeroom for tapes and microfilms and –

ME-N: And pleasant memories! Look, there's Pepper, the first dog we ever had, the one the milkman ran over. And there's our pet raccoon that disappeared when he was two and we were fifty-two.

*(Out of some dormitory of pet memories tumble all the pets we ever had, and the whole kit and caboodle of us roll and romp in dog-cat-raccoon-human ecstasy. It is Me-R who calls us all to order.)*

ME-R: Stop! Stop! We must not forget why we came here. If the pets will sit quietly with us, they may stay.

*(Which they do, and somehow they unstiffen the stiffness which would have been had my several selves sat in a circle in my subliminal self without them. Me-N could never have sat so still so long had Raccoon not steathily been going through all her pockets all the while.)*

ME-R: How did he do it? What really happened?

ME-T: We are faced with the theological task of expounding the doctrine of God's Grace.

ME-E *(She would have leaped to her feet had the fat black puppy not been on her lap.):* No, no, a thousand times no! It's an existential task to spell out Grace in my life right now, this day, this hour, this minute! Our concept of Grace is too cramped and narrow.

ME-T *(grimly):* Your concept of theology is too cramped and narrow!

ME-R: Well, where do we begin?

ME-I: *(tickling a kitten's stomach):* Life is real and life is earnest –.

ME-T: Don't be silly!

ME-R: You are not as funny as you think!

ME-E: Despair, my stumbling block, my other self, why don't you start us off. Epitomize the mood of today.

ME-D: All I have to do is paint you my own! Joylessness, boredom, disgust, nausea. Life is a humbug, a cruel joke. Existence is a prison.

42

ME-R: It's just sin at work! Now if only there were more Christians . . .!

ME-D: Sorry, Madame Respectable! I'm tired of being such a monster of negativity, but these Christians who take a cocksure stance about a guaranteed happiness in an eternal future and live in their present like moles in their tunnels have created more cynics than so-called free-thinkers ever did. The Christians who are afraid of being joyous, happy laughing creatures in the here-and-now have created a greater credibility gap between believers and unbelievers than unbelievers ever could.

ME-R: I know lots of happy Christians!

ME-E: No you don't, not really! You know a lot of Christians who feel good and virtuous and even saintly about themselves by doing the only thing anyone can ever do to feel good and virtuous and even saintly about himself.

ME-I: What's that? Tell me. I want to feel good and virtuous and even saintly.

ME-E: Take the vastness and the fullness of God's requirement for man, cut it down, peel and pare it down to size, to man's pitiful puny, selfish size – and then obey that scrap, that mite, that grub of a requirement with all one's might. But obedience to that tiny dab is disobedience. Feeling good about it is blasphemy.

ME-I: Ouch!

ME-R *(whispering):* Even our good is no good!

ME-N: Oh, oh! We're lurching toward bankruptcy!

ME-I *(suddenly serious):* I wonder how many times I have discovered my good to be no good! The worst was to have my cozy rug of social and political optimism pulled from under me. I used to put so much stock and hope in this new passion to be honest and relevant, in the passionate hatred of mediocrity, hypocrisy, and complacency. But it didn't take long to discover that the new passion to be honest and relevant creates new hypocrisies and new complacencies and mediocrity as totally tyrannical as the old mediocrity.

ME-D: The old evil always comes back in new forms!

ME-T *(almost shouting. She is making a connection!):* "Hell, we'll never get away from rhythm. The bad stuff keeps coming back, and it's the worst rhythm there is!" Saul Bellow had Henderson say that in *Henderson the Rain King.* And it's true, true, true! That's good Christian theology! And I'm just beginning to see the comedy of it. I think there's a great big belly-laughing "Ha! Ha!" in the doctrine of Original Sin! Be quiet, all of you, I think I'm having a revelation!

*(Me-T buries her face in our old Angora cat's fur, and my astounded selves are so quiet that we can hear Princess purring. When Me-T raises her head again, her face is crinkled with laughter.)*

ME-T: It's outlandish. It's preposterous. It's as absurd and as radical as anything I've ever known, but I think there's truth in it. I think this is part of what he was trying to tell us – namely, to wit, to wit . . . *(Me-T pauses to liberate some very untheological chuckles)* . . .

The best is the worst
>    Hallelujah!
The worst is the best
>    Hallelujah!

ME-R *(genuinely bewildered):* I don't get it!

ME-T *(looking and talking amazingly like Ecstasy):* Grace, sweet Grace, amazing Grace – it doesn't just start when we feel loved and cleansed and forgiven, like a baby that's had its soiled diaper removed, has been bathed, wrapped up warm and snug in a clean blanket, and held close in loving arms to its mother's breast. That's not when Grace, sweet Grace, amazing Grace, begins at all! Oh, no, not at all! *(Me-T leans forward dramatically.)* It begins way back there in that old-fashioned, austere, uncompromising Christian doctrine of Original Sin – the most painful view of man, the worst view of man ever concocted. Some people think it a colossal embarrassment. Some call it a man-diminishing calamity, a huge minus that has thrown the psyche of Western man out of joint. But it's the *best!* The worst view of man is the best!

ME-D: My fortress of despair was really rocked by the Juggler last night, and your excitement is touching, but you still don't communicate how it is possible to say:

Life is horror – hallelujah!
Man is evil – hallelujah!
I am bad – hallelujah!

And to call it Grace is absurd!

ME-T: Of course it's absurd! It's the Divine Comedy, the Divine Theater of the Absurd! But one leaves *this* theater in Grace and not disgrace! Grace is accepting "the worst." Grace is to know the worst in man and to know that the worst in man is possible in me. Ho, ho, ho! You can't shock me! *I know it all.* You're not telling me a thing about man and about me. I have no illusions about me and none about man, none whatsoever! Grace is to accept life completely. Not to take a moral holiday, not to lose sight of the horror, not to pull down the blinds of the mind, *but* – to accept the worst. Having accepted the worst, there's no further shock. There's nothing worse to fear. You know the worst and lose fright of the horror.

ME-D *(releasing a long sigh):* That's great, that's tremendous! Down with painful self-scrutiny! Who said it: "Rake the muck this way, rake the muck that way, still muck!" No more living on the defensive. No more tense watching, watching, brooding, and worrying and wondering what's coming next on the human scene, paralyzed with remorse for the past, guilt for the present, and fear of the future. No more despair, for you know the rock-bottom, the ultimate despair, you know the worst. Oh, Me-T, it's an exuberant thought!

ME-E *(recovering her role as the Ecstatic):* And it clears the decks, Hallelujah! Think of the waste, the waste of vital energies, the wear and tear on the human psyche, of disillusioned optimism, shattered idealism, disabling pessimism, and paralyzing cynicism! Think of the woman-hours wasted trying to build up one's self-image by tearing down others. Think of the man-hours wasted denouncing everybody and everything under the sun.

ME-I: The next time we meet that man we call Chief Jawbone of the Dia-Tribe I'm going to stop him smack in the middle of his harangue and chant:

Ho! ho! ho!
You may stop right now,
for I know it all.
I know the worst,
the worst there's to know.

*(Having accepted the worst, having learned that there really is nothing fearful in this place because they already know the fearful things hiding there, my several selves decide as one to go back upstairs. "Why don't you come up there and play with us?" they ask their recollected pets. "You never summon us," they say. "We will, we will! But come by yourselves sometimes and surprise us in our dreams." "We will," they say.)*

enter

søren kierkegaard

act ɪᴠ

*He is pacing Dialectical Hall from stem to stern when my six several selves burst in chattering animatedly, a man "of lean body and visage as if his eager soul, biting for anger at the clog of his body, desired to fret a passage through it." On seeing all my Me's he stops his pacing and gesticulates peremptorily with his cane.*

SOREN KIERKEGAARD: Too many women! I hate babbling, gabbling women!
*(Whereupon my six Me's promptly nucleate and I stand there a Corporate Me, an I, alone with him. I know him at once, of course, not so much for*

49

*his bushy hair, the aristocratic curve of his nose, the slight askewness of his shoulders that makes him walk obliquely, but for the amazing liveliness of his eyes and mobility of his features. Our eyes meet and take each other's soundings.)*

I: You were full of contrasting selves, too, you know, only you called them pseudonyms, and you situated your true self somewhere between your antitheses, Johannes Climacus and Anti-Climacus, but I suspect that the man Søren Kierkegaard filled the whole space between them, and even that space was not enough.

s.k. *(a chuckling infectious laugh shaking his whole body):* You have been spying on me!

I: As you spied on everybody! Oh, you played many roles – Kierkegaard the spy, Kierkegaard the gadfly, Kierkegaard the whip. You made a whip of men's pleasant vices and scourged them unmercifully.

s.k.: Which one did you summon when you summoned me here?

I: Kierkegaard, the teacher and preacher of the Grace of God.

s.k. *(genuinely startled):* I have not often been labelled so graciously!

I: The Hymn to Grace is pretty hard to find in, with, and under the lampooning of men.

s.k.: Yet all that I said that they said and say was bad was only to reach an Alleluia.

I: And only because you believed in the Grace of God, leaned toward the Grace of God, grabbed at the Grace of God, caught and clung to the Grace of God.

s.k.: Yes, of course, what else?

I: You flashed across my mind down there – I must say that you came quickly – when I began to feel that we were getting too exuberant. Sometimes exuberance leads to disheveled thinking. There is enough confusion as there is about Grace without our adding to the jumble.

s.k.: If you do not move on from your understanding of the prevalence of sin – Yes, I overheard what you were saying. One of the benefits, you see –. If you do not move on from your understanding that the world is drenched in sin, you will certainly bog down in a very popular confusion. It is easy, almost cozy, to confess total, universal, collective guilt. The painful thing is to trace the connection between that huge conglomerate body of sin to yourself as a single individual before God. The wrenching thing is to change a generality into a particularity. The agony is to change people into eaches, to introduce the "I", to switch from "they" or "we" to "I."

i: David's agony all over again! His anger at "the man who had done this" and the prophet Nathan's *You* are the man!" – and then that tremendous cry from his anguished conscience:

> Have mercy on me, O God according to thy stead-fast love; according to thy abundant mercy blot out my transgressions. Wash me thoroughly from my iniquity, and cleanse me from my sin! For I know my transgression, and my sin is ever before me. Against thee, thee only have I sinned.

s.k.: The anguished conscience! It is a painful road to travel from the general to the particular, from the impersonal to the personal, from "they" and "we" to "I". Do you wish to take it?

i: Of course, if it ends in Grace.

s.k. *(sharply):* Madame, it is Grace all the way! The consciousness of sin, the anguished conscience, is not the gate to Grace, it *is* the Grace of God. No one who approaches God from any other standpoint than that of his own moral imperfection will ever know the height and the breadth and the depth of God's love. To wish to come to God by any other way is treason against Christianity! The anguished conscience understands Christianity. Remove the anguished conscience and you may as well lock the churches and convert them into dance halls.

ı: There are a goodly number of people, even some who call themselves Christian theologians, who are saying that these days – that the churches should be locked and converted into dance halls. They say that the Christian church has lost its relevance.

s.k.: The Christian church will be relevant as long as man is suspended between ideal perfection and the imperfectness of existential life.

ı: But they have abolished all infinite ideals, all absolutes. They say that everything is relative.

s.k.: So it has come, then – the age of diluted social morality! I predicted it – that the absolute of the new age would be that everything is relative. But tell me, is there no anxiety any more? Has abolishing absolutes abolished anxiety, melancholy, despair? Are men more relaxed, more satisfied, cheerful, and tranquil now that they are relevant and simply compare modes and methods, procedures and processes? Has man gained status and stature by comparing himself only with other men? Has his self esteem gained by it? Is he gay, this modern man liberated from God's expectation for a man? Is he dancing for joy because he no longer lives on God's terms but on man's?

ı: Don't ask *me*, Mr. Kierkegaard! One hundred and twenty-five years ago you yourself predicted the state of mind of our age with amazing accuracy.

s.k.: There is no escaping anxiety over the human predicament. If all the religions of all the nations and peoples of all the ages were put into a big pot and simmered down to their most basic basic state of mind and most basic basic goal, they would be:

State of mind: Anxiety – there is something wrong.

Goal: We must find a solution.

I: How true! The ancient Hawaiians betrayed that anxiety and that quest for a solution when they tried to make sure they did not ignore any one of the gods and addressed them thus:

> O long god
> O short god
> O god breathing in short sibilant breaths
> O god blowing like the whistling winds
> O god watching, peeping at one
> O god hiding, slipping out of sight
> O all ye gods who travel on the dark night's path,
> Come eat.

s.k.: Trying to get rid of anxiety by getting rid of right and wrong judgments is no solution. Indeed, any attempt to do that leads to ever more terrible and destructive forms of sin. Man gains stature as man by knowing *that* infinitely much is expected of him, by knowing *how infinitely much* is expected of him, by *knowing* it.

I: So I find out who I am by finding out who I ought to be?

s.k.: Splendid! For a woman you –

I: None of your deprecatory remarks about women, please! It is not tolerated today. Nor should it be! It really was inexcusable of you, Sir!

53

s.k.: Like a woman you change the subject.

i: *You* did! You inserted the subject of women.

s.k.: If you start that womanish "You did!" "you didn't!" business, I shall leave.

i: You will not! I have you conned, so to speak. I am going to keep you prisoner in my thought until you help me think through this "anguished conscience" bit. It still seems so far from Grace!

*(He does not seem to mind being detained, and I am not sure it is against his will either, for he had always loved an argument. "Dialectical" was one of his favorite words. Indeed, it seems as if he feels at home here, as if he thinks he is pacing rapidly about his own apartment in Nørregade, sifting and sorting the barrage of ideas that dart into his head from Lord knows where.)*

i: You see, Sir, I refuse to believe in my daily self. I, too, have lost all my illusions about myself. First I lost the happy illusions of childhood.

I'm happy, happy, happy as can be,
and I love you God for making me.
I love you as much –
as much as I love my teddy-bear.

Puppy chewed up my teddy-bear, and I hated God. Next I lost the beautiful illusions of youth.

God, lovely God, I know you have
something incredibly lovely around
the next corner for me – just for me!

54

Around the next corner was the Big Depression of the '30s – teaching eight grades and thirty-five undisciplined kids in a one-room rural school in northern Wisconsin at the age of seventeen.

But, good Sir, I don't want to bore you with autobiographical whimpering and whining. Nor would a catalog of lost illusions make a true picture, for life has been incredibly good to me. But, here, one of your most loyal admirers and best translators, David Swenson, said the "lost illusion" bit very well:

> Faith in the eternal arises like the phoenix out of the ashes of all the soul's previous illusions. It supersedes not only the happy illusions of childhood and the beautiful illusions of youth, the illusions of a romantic love that is happiness without responsibility; the illusions of maturity, which center about fame and money, power and success; but also the most persistent and deep-seated of all illusions, the illusion of self-adequacy and self-righteousness.

I can honestly say that I have lost all those illusions. I have no trouble with illusions – unless, perhaps, my thinking that I have no illusions is an illusion!

And I also know that there is no place for vanity underneath my to-the-visible-eye admirably well-organized, well-functioning, well-rewarding life. Furthermore, I also know, as Shakespeare put it in *Macbeth,* we must "raze out the written troubles of the brain, cleanse the stuffed bosom of that perilous stuff which weighs upon the heart." But – and here is the nub of the matter – *do we always need to be watching the movements of the inner being?* Do we always have to have that Old Testament God thundering behind and before, to the left and to the right: "You shall and you shan't, you will and you won't, you're damned if you do and damned if you don't!" All this constant self-scrutinizing leads to an anguished conscience, but do we want that, do we need that? Doesn't the anguished conscience end in despair, a paralysis of despair that is far, far worse than this general uneasiness about the predicament of man, this anxiety about something being wrong?

*(I stop, amazed that I have held forth so long, but more amazed that he has permitted me to.)*

s.k.: I agree, I agree, and didn't I say it many times? There is nothing more dangerous, more paralyzing than a certain isolating self-scrutiny where one sits and constantly stares at his own navel, and one's whole life, all one's relationships, become infected with self, poisoned by self. But this is not true at all of the self-scrutiny before God, where one discovers that even his human pluperfectness is imperfect. Anguished conscience before God, yes – provisional and partial – but it is not a shameful secret, a humiliating embarrassment. Indeed, to the contrary, it becomes a kind of joke between you and God. You make no bones about it. You admit it, you make a clean and honest admission. You need God, you need Grace. You will always need God, you will always need Grace. You will need Grace to receive Grace. Indeed, Madame, I wrote a discourse on this and entitled it "Man's Perfection Is His Need of God." God's judgment upon you is a good and perfect gift. Your imperfection is a good and perfect gift. Your guilt is a good and perfect gift. How else would you know that you had hurt or failed love? Your despair is a good and perfect gift. It teaches you not only to take refuge in Grace but also how to live in Grace, make use of Grace. It leads you to the Alleluia.

It would be the saddest of tragedies to pass through life and not discover that you need God, need Grace. The moment you go naked out of your self-scrutiny before God as you did formerly from the womb, it becomes a Divine Comedy.

Grace, you see, is never a substitute for the anguished conscience, for repentance. Self-knowledge of one's nothingness created the condition which allows God to dwell in you. The joke is that one can boast without blushing, as Paul did. To speak of God's Grace is to speak indirectly of one's own nothingness, unworthiness. The joke is that one's nothingness is one's greatness.

And you are afraid that the anguished conscience leads to a perpetual paralysis of despair! Oh, Madame, it leads to saints, for what are saints but weak things filled with the boundless Grace of God!

*(And then it happens. I cannot help it. Me-E, my Ecstasy, slips out of my Corporate Me and dances up to Kierkegaard.)*

ME-E: You wonderful, wonderful Danes! You make hymns to man's predicament. I modernized one of your Danish hymns once. You make me remember it.

CONGRUOUS INCONGRUITY

You, Peace Prophet to my contentiousness
You, Absolute addressed to my deficiency
You, Divine Anticipation of my predicament
You, God's Son!

You with YES, I with NO
You assenting, I denying
You with Grace for my disgrace
You a Savior, I a sinner

Ah, how we two fit!
How you dovetail my jaggedness!
How you reconcile my irreconcilables!
How you complete my incompleteness!

Truth for my untruth
Vine in my wasteland
Door out of my self-enclosure
Thou – my Christ!

*(Nor can I prevent what happens next. Kierkegaard comes toward us with eyes flashing and cane upraised. Me-E quickly slips back into my Corporate Me.)*

S.K.: Are you a poet?

I: No, Sir, I merely write prose that sometimes strains at the leash.

S.K. *(still in a rage):* The last thing I wanted, the thing I feared most, was to fall into the hands of professors and poets, that scurvy crowd that do not exist in the truths they write about with beautiful words, that bunch of leeches that live on the sufferings of others! I will not have it, I tell you, I will not have it!

*(Just then there is a loud knocking at the door, and in comes the man I hastily summon – just in time! The cane clatters to the floor, and Søren stands there stunned.)*

58

luther confronts

kierkegaard

act v

*Even though I know that Kierkegaard once called Luther another Copernicus, I am wholly unprepared for his first words to the latest visitor to Dialectical Hall. Recovering quickly from his initial surprise, Kierkegaard bows deeply, as a subject to his king.*

S.K.: Ah, Luther, you are still the master of us all!

LUTHER *(It is the Cranach Luther, strong, swarthy, and with eyes that can see personal and private devils as well as God. His laughter delivers me from every tension.):* Aha! That depends! What am I master of – all the simpletons, the rogues, the apostates, the demagogues, the opportunists?

s.k. *(quietly):* You are master of all who have tried in their time to reintroduce Christianity into Christendom.

LUTHER: You mean us meddlers with the Establishment! But the Holy Spirit is the greatest meddler of us all. *(Turns to me with a look that embraces my full womanhood and makes me understand why a young woman with a warm heart and warm blood would throw her life into his life for better or for worse.)* And you, Madame, are you one of us busybodies?

I: Oh, no, Sir! I am – well, you could call me a student of Grace. I need you two to help me because you have had such profound insights.

LUTHER: If I have profound insights, Madame, it is because I have often experienced profound spiritual assault. *Anfechtung* it is called in German.

s.k.:*Anfægtelse* in Danish. But it is one and the same, and I, too, had many an attack.

I: Is it what we call mental depression today?

LUTHER: It's an unholy combination of the three damned D's: Doubt, Depression, Despair.

I *(dismayed):* Do you mean that even the great ones fall in and out of Grace? Do you mean that Grace is a capricious thing?

LUTHER: The relation of the New Man to God in Christ is no capricious thing, but the Old Man continues to hang around and get in his licks. To say it in my dear old familiar tongue: *der alte Adam uns immer am Halse hängen bleibt.* But where my New Man is not altogether trustworthy and unchanging, my God *is!*

*(Kierkegaard, meanwhile, is becoming strangely excited and fiercely determined. He muzzles the two of us with his brilliant eyes and snubs any further exploration of the not-so-easy doctrine of Blessed Assurance.)*

s.k.: You, Madame, seem to have a strong will. Will us a carriage and horses.

With such a visitor as this we cannot stay cooped up in this matronage. Besides, you have not offered us a thing to eat, and Luther has taken a firm stand against fasting. I shall take you to eat at my favorite inn north of Copenhagen.

I: I can, if you will, think you a Cadillac or a jet –

S.K.: Fie on your modern inventions! Subjectivity is truth, and your modern inventions are objectivity incarnate. And I thought railroads were bad! *(So, in an open carriage, with a reckless driver and a team of frisky horses, we drive through the beech forests of North Zealand. However, I am unable to give my attention to the rapid dialog between Luther and Kierkegaard – I think it is about Aristotle – until I let Me-I, Me-E, and Me-N escape to play all day in the hushed and hidden forest. With only the three more theologically-minded Me's remaining, I am able to concentrate on my hosts. I may have invited them into my brain-house, but it is they, I assure you, who take me out to dinner! The conversation does not turn to Grace until we sit down in a delightful, secluded inn to roast duck, sweet-sour red cabbage, and piping hot nut-brown potatoes as small as crockery marbles. It is Luther who turns us back to Grace.)*

LUTHER *(busily packing a cargo of potatoes, cabbage, and duck on the back of his fork, European style):* The Lord Jesus Christ likes none but the hungry and thirsting souls. The gorged and glutted souls do not need his food. It is need, Madame, that laps up Grace. The more need, the more Grace.

I: But why are we not lapping up Grace today?

S.K.: Because you have changed the doctrine of the forgiveness of sins in Christ Jesus to the doctrine of permission of sins.

LUTHER *(mildly surprised):* Seems to me I said that once –.

S.K.: You did! It is one of your better statements. No, Madame, you and your generation are in the pitiable state of having a bland and lenient God who winks at sin and a Jesus who has climbed down from the cross to be your Big Brother and not your Savior, for you do not need a Savior and you do not need Grace. Who laps up what he does not need?

I: How did it happen?

S.K.: You botched up Grace, that's how! You somehow got the silly notion that our Lord God has become a doddering old man who doesn't know what's going on! But if our Lord God was ever an old man, it was in the Old Testament – laying down the Law, seeing that it wasn't fulfilled and scolding, punishing, and all that. The Lord God became young in the New Testament where he stepped down to earth and walked among men. It's like a new teacher coming to a school and taking over from the old scolding rigorous teacher. The new teacher makes the concession of infinite gentleness, infinite love, and the whole school is reborn, rejuvenated.

LUTHER: Don't pass over the "infinite concession of gentleness and love" so lightly, so swiftly! Or that it was the same God who made it!

> Who will deliver me from this body of death? Thanks be to God through Jesus Christ our Lord! . . . there is therefore now no condemnation for those who are in Christ Jesus. For the law of the Spirit of life in Christ Jesus has set me free from the law of sin and death.

S.K.: My point is that Grace is more rigorous than the Law, and this woman's generation does not see that. Face to face with Grace a person really learns to know what lies deepest in him. Tell a child to do something – that doesn't mean the child does it, but whether he does or doesn't, you really do not get to know the child's true nature. But say, "You are free, do what you want" – *then* you find out the deep down nature of the child!

A rigorous proclamation of the Law can demoralize man, but the most dangerous demoralization is and remains the demoralization brought about by the misuse of Grace. And you, Martin Luther, you bear a grave responsibility for that! You gave men the slogan "Faith alone, Grace alone" – and they, weary of their austere diet of work-righteousness, ate it up and stuffed themselves fat and lazy with "Faith alone, Grace alone" – and got thoroughly constipated.

It is not just sheer accident, Martin Luther, that the divorce between thought and action is most prevalent and conspicious in Lutheran countries. Your emphasis on "Faith alone, Grace alone" became a fig leaf for shirking. *(At this Luther pushes his plate away so violently that the little marble potatoes roll onto the table and from there to the floor, and the battle begins. The words fly – I half expect dishes to. I cannot even begin to reproduce the exuberant truculence of the language of the two men!)*

LUTHER: In the heat of battle a man never thinks of the outcome – either of his victory or of his defeat. In my battle with the Pope I did not foresee two possible outcomes and extremes: cheap Grace – or Grace made into a new kind of Law. You, Søren Kierkegaard, apparently have made the free gift of God's Grace into an ultimatum more horrible than the Pope's!

s.k.: And you, Martin Luther, you toppled the Pope and set the Public on the throne, and the Public proceeded to make your doctrine of Faith alone, Grace alone, into the doctrine of the Big Rock Candy Mountain.

LUTHER: Never, never did I forbid the Christian man to do good works, and any man who charges me with that is a son of Beelzebub. I simply said that if man rests on merits and works, he does not rest on God's Grace and mercy. If he rests on God's Grace and mercy, he does not rest on merits and works.

I *(with unseemly excitement):* Don't you see, Mr. Kierkegaard? It's the same as *your* Either/Or!

s.к. *(icily): My* Either/Or, Madame, corrected the serious deficiency in Luther's Either/Or. My Either/Or is: either to *exist* in the Truth/or to hold merely to a set of bald propositions. The trouble with you, Luther, was that you were muddle-headed. You were not a dialectician. You always saw only one side of the issue.

You did indeed and rightly so set "Faith alone, Grace alone" in its rightful place, but you also made a place for wine, women, and cards – and the whole pack of human self-indulgences. You made Grace itself an indulgence, and to memorialize you we ought to put your face on a deck of cards as the jack-of-clubs!

*(Luther is speechless with rage, indeed, looks apoplectic-purple. And I – I am ashamed to say I resort to womanish ways and screech.)*

I: *Tie stille! (Kierkegaard is amazed to be told to shut up in his own language.)* Quit blaming Luther for what the generations after him did to politicize, secularize, and nullify his principle of Grace! Do we blame *you* for what has been done the last hundred years to your principle of existing in the Truth? Do we blame you for Heidegger? Good heavens, man, you despised systems, and he has systematized your existentialism into an atheistic *Existenzphilosophie!* Do we blame you for Jean-Paul Sartre? Do we blame you for every unkempt intellectual tramp roaming around muttering "I am an existentialist! I am an existentialist!"

*(Kierkegaard abruptly leaves the table, walks to a window looking out to the beech forest, and stands with his back to us. Luther sinks back in his*

*chair and glumly and grimly resumes eating. I can only sit there and frantically wonder, "What next? What next?" I could send the two packing, banish them from my mind, but something-yet-to-be-resolved makes me keep them there. As abruptly as he has left us, Kierkegaard returns and stands before Luther, his demeanor once again that of a disciple before his master.)*

s.k.: Forgive me, Luther! I stand by your principle of "Faith alone." Your concept of Grace is infinitely lofty, infinitely costly. You came to it after great spiritual trials. You came to it from the anguished conscience. It was the secular mentality that seized it quickly and made it a solid bourgeois Lutheran home for indolence and inaction. I have only tried to jack up the price again, to make it what you so clearly saw it to be. Forgive me!

*(And Luther, bless him, that splendidly generous soul, who may not have been a dialectical genius but far exceeded Kierkegaard when it came to acquitting his opponents and enemies of their sins of disagreement, Luther stands up and encloses not one but both of Kierkegaard's hands in his great peasant paws.)*

LUTHER: I said it before, and I say it again – the world is like a drunken peasant. If one helps him up on one side of the horse, he falls off on the other side.

*(Once again they sit down to enjoy hugely their Danish dinner, and I to enjoy hugely their dialog.)*

s.k.: You were quite right in distinguishing between Christ as gift and Christ as pattern. You were confronted by the exaggerated misuse of Christ as pattern and moved in the direction of Christ as gift. I was confronted with the exaggerated misuse of Christ as gift and moved in the direction of Christ as pattern.

LUTHER: To use Christ *rightly* as gift and to use Christ *rightly* as pattern – neither diminishes the Grace of God. It is all Grace, the bare goodness of God, the gift of Christ's total self to our total selves.

S.K. *(still on the defensive):* Remember that I lived in the 19th century, a time of optimism, enterprise, progress, and perfectibility. I stressed Christ as pattern to humble men, to put them on a collision course, for one who lives and loves and acts as Christ wants us to live and love and act inevitably collides with the world. I used the imitation of Christ dialectically to train the need for Grace, to prevent Christianity from becoming mythology, and to maintain justice ethically. The social morality of this woman's age *(he nods at me)* does not drive her to Grace. She no doubt fulfills the requirements of social morality tolerably well.

ME-IMP *(invisible inside of the Corporate Me but still audible!):*

Little Jack Horner
sat in a corner
eating his social-morality pie.
He put in his thumb
and pulled out a plum
and said, "What a nice,
good, proper, exemplary,
moral, upright boy am I!"

I *(speaking somewhat loudly to cover up for Me-I, not wanting another scene with S.K.):* But how could you chide any man for slighting good and gracious works who said,

It is as absurd and stupid to say: the righteous ought to do good works, as to say: God ought to do good, the sun ought to shine, the pear tree ought to bear pears, three and seven ought to be ten; for all this follows of necessity by reason of the cause and the consequence . . . it all follows without commandment or bidding of any law, naturally and willingly, uncompelled and unconstrained . . . the sun shines by nature, unbidden; the pear tree bears pears of itself, uncompelled; three and seven ought not to be ten, they are ten already. There is no need to say to our Lord God that he ought to do good; for he does it without ceasing, of himself, willingly and with pleasure. Just so, we do not have to tell the righteous that he ought to do good works, for he does so without that, without any commandment or compulsion, because he is a new creature and a good tree.

*(Even before the quotation is finished, Kierkegaard's eyes twinkle and his face has an almost roguish look.)*

s.k.: *Der alte Adam uns immer am Halse hängen bleibt!* You see, Madame, Luther sometimes contradicted himself.

luther *(interrupting amiably):* There is always room for contradictions in Grace!

s.k.: I did not have misgivings about Grace Alone or Luther or Lutheranism. My only misgiving was about myself, for I knew that I was not the Lord God. I knew that that cunning fellow, my self-seeking self, still hung around my neck and would seek every way to take that beautiful gift of Grace in vain and make it a blind for a nice easy untroubled bourgeois life. That is my reason for tightening the screws a bit on that concept.

LUTHER: *(comfortably):* I truly do believe that we – you, too, Madame – are good Augustinians. He told us, you remember, that Grace is given not because we have done good works, but in order that we may be able to do them – that is, not because we have fulfilled the Law, but that we may be enabled to do so.

*(The rest of the evening is so undiscordant that I find myself drawing my tremendous enjoyment – not from the conversation – but from watching Luther and Kierkegaard enjoying each other's company and the food. They greet the marzipan cake and rich Danish coffee with uninhibited enthusiasm, laugh and talk without restraint. However, there are still many questions in my mind, and we part company promising to meet each other at Gillelei the next day. I am too keyed up with the wine of ideas to sleep, and it is a relief to have Me-I, Me-E, and Me-N slip back into my head, one by one. Each one shyly gives me a poem, and I finally fall asleep in a beech forest where the trees are proud host and ancient friend to moss and lichen, the guests who stayed so long that guest and host are fused, and beech is green and green is beech until one almost expects the heart-grain to be stained green, the mist-green, the lyrical green, the tender, unsophisticated green green green . . .)*

amazing grace

act VI

*Kierkegaard is alone at Gilleleie when I arrive the next day, refreshed by sleep and with all my Me's firmly in custody in my head. My three recalcitrants capitulated when Me-T told them that if they found the conversation lustreless and dull, they at least would have the sea, the sea, the sea – and when Me-E remembered Melville's words:*

> "There is, one knows not what sweet mystery about this sea, whose gently awful stirrings seem to speak of some hidden soul beneath."

*Gilleleie, a small fishing village on the north coast of Zealand, about twenty miles west of Helsingør, faces on the Kattegat. It was one of Kierkegaard's favorite haunts, and a huge boulder on the sand dunes memorializes his solitary walks along the coast, watching the wind pulsate the immense surface of the sea or lash it into foam and flying spray. Chiselled into the stone are lines Kierkegaard wrote into his Journal on August 1, 1835, at the age of 22:*

> The thing is to find a truth which is true *for me,* to find *the idea for which I can live or die.*

*When Kierkegaard craved the human scene, he sat on a green bench in the village watching the fishermen mending the nets or going and coming in their deep-keeled fishing boats. The green bench is still there, and it is here I find Kierkegaard, sunk in silence. I have to prod him into dialog.*

1: Those fishing boats with keels as deep as their superstructures remind me of what a melancholy contemporary of mine, Cyril Connolly, said about unhappiness:

> I understand how valuable unhappiness can be; melancholy and remorse form the deep leaden keel which enables us to sail into the world of reality; we run aground sooner than the flat bottomed pleasure lovers, but we venture out in weather that will sink them, and we choose our direction. What distinguishes true civilization from the man-fabricated substitutes except that tap-root to the unconscious, the sense of original sin.

s.k. *(a bit irritably):* Is it unhappiness you want to pick my mind about today?

i: Well, not, not really. Happiness, perhaps, a certain zest for life, joy –

s.k.: Ah, you are just like all the rest, looking for a special kind of beatitude in your Christianity. The true gospel is in conflict with most of the systems, customs, and attitudes of any and every age, and conflict does not beget beatitude!

i: I don't aim that high – beatitude. I would be content with a sense of festivity in life, a real sense of joy.

s.k.: Oh, the harm Christian preachers have done by having to do it up big at the very beginning and proclaiming Christianity as joy, joy, joy!

*(By this time Me-Despair is putting up such a fuss that I have to let her speak. In fact, I find it necessary to dissolve into my several selves and let them speak.)*

me-d: Stop your damned masculine intellectual sparring! What I want is to be cured of my self-loathing, this ill will toward myself.

s.k. *(looking at Despair keenly):* Ah, one of these "deep natures"!

me-d *(angrily, for she hears the cynical quotation marks):* Meaning?

s.k.: One of these "deep natures" which says: "Christ died for the sins of the whole world, but not for mine. He died for all, but not for me. I am more sincere and intense than the ordinary soul. I take my sins seriously." God may forgive them, but they cannot forgive themselves.

*(Me-D falls into a flustered silence, and Kierkegaard to his credit promptly abandons his sarcasm.)*

s.k.: Believe me, Madame, if I recognize your despair, it is because I myself fought it so long – long after I believed that God had forgiven my sins in Christ. It was a long time before I dared to forgive myself, dared to forget my guilt, dared to stop that morbid paralyzing kind of self-scrutiny that destroys the self. In fact, I wrote a book about my despair and called it *The Sickness unto Death,* the sin of despairing over one's sin.

The direction of your particular distress – I cannot forgive myself – is *away* from God, *away* from Grace. In fact, it is a defiance, a refusing to believe in forgiveness. It takes you deeper and deeper into self-loathing. You sink deeper and deeper into despair.

ME-D: You know! You know! But how does one rise! How does one ascend?

S.K.: By accepting Grace *also for me,* by accepting the forgiveness of sins *also for me.* By daring to believe it. By daring to forgive yourself for what God has already forgiven you.

ME-D.: But *how?*

S.K.: By a leap of faith.

ME-E: Oh, Despair, why is it so hard for you to do what all the rest of us have already done? All you do is to say, "Christ died for the sins of the world!" and take a big long run . . . and shout "And for me – e – e – e – e – e!" and land on the other side – on the Grace-side.

ME-T: Bravo, Ecstasy, you are becoming a theologian!

ME-R: Surprisingly orthodox, too!

S.K.: The essential task for the individual in the forgiveness of sins is to make it valid in time. It is the new creation. When the pastor says, "I declare unto you the gracious forgiveness of all your sins," he does not mean forgiveness some time, he means forgiveness now.

ME-D *(whispering):* The gracious forgiveness of all my sins! The gracious forgiveness of all my sins! Mine! My despair. . . .

S.K.: My tragedy was that I stalled so long before I accepted the *also for me.* One does not forgive himself until he accepts that *also for me.*

76

ME-D: If you had dared to believe that sooner, would you have married Regine?

S.K.: Yes, If I had forgiven myself sooner for what God had already forgiven me, I could have married Regine. *(He is silent for a time, and there is only the sound of the sea gulls screaming in the harbor where the fishermen are cleaning their catch.)*

S.K.: When the thought of God no longer reminds one of his sin but that it is forgiven, and the past is no longer the memory of how much wrong one has done but of how much he has been forgiven, then a man is resting in the forgiveness of sins, resting in Grace.

*(A hearty laugh makes us all turn to see Luther striding toward us, his black robes flapping in the wind off the sea.)*

LUTHER *(clapping S.K. on his thin shoulders):* Aha, my friend, now I caught *you* in a self-contradiction! You who are always declaring that faith is a restless thing and that Luther's doctrine of faith alone, Grace alone makes men lie down and do nothing – you just said that man *rests* in the forgiveness of sins, *rests* in Grace. You said it yourself – *rests!* That means, my friend, that he takes refuge in Grace, relaxes in Grace, breathes freely in Grace, has confidence before God and before men. Yes, by the Grace of God, he has confidence in himself!

ME-I *(impishly):* Even-Stephen! Even-Stephen!

ME-R: Shh! Have you no respect?

S.K.: Madame, the particular kind of confidence we receive in Grace gives us a mental playfulness called humor. *(To Luther)* As for you, *touché!* But what you say only affirms my point that Grace, too, is dialectical and has a thousand tongues. However, you do agree that Grace does not cause men to ride at anchor in some safe harbor. Grace, properly preached, pushes man out into 70,000 fathoms of water, out into the storms of life, where he discovers every day in every way his desperate need for Grace.

LUTHER: But one rides secure! One rides secure! You are a Dane, and the sea provides your imagery. I am a German peasant, and the farm provides mine. I think of wagons, the wagons of Joseph, the wagons Joseph sent to carry his father and brothers back to the abundance in Egypt.

It is just as difficult for us to believe that such great blessings have been conferred on us unworthy creatures in Christ Jesus as it was for Jacob to believe that his son Joseph was alive and was governor of Egypt. In Genesis 45 we read that Jacob was like one awakened out of deep slumber and did not believe his sons *until they showed him the wagons of Joseph.*

Ah, it is a good wagon God has made for us in Christ Jesus: righteousness and sanctification and redemption and wisdom.

As Paul said in Corinthians 1: For I am a sinner, yet I am drawn in his righteousness, which is given me. I am unclean, but his holiness is my sanctification, in which I pleasurably ride. I am an ignorant fool, but his wisdom carries me forward. I have deserved condemnation, but I am set free by his redemption, a wagon in which I sit secure!

S.K.: Splendid! Splendid! How did I miss that! But the wagon carries me *forward,* not backward!

LUTHER: Indeed, indeed! And the wagon may even burn up the road at times. And the heart, man, ah, the heart that has experienced that God is a God who looks into the depths and helps the poor, despised, afflicted, miserable, forsaken, and those who are nothing – there, in that heart is born a hearty love for God, and the heart overflows with gladness and goes leaping and dancing for the great pleasure it has found in God.

ME-E *(leaping up, clapping her hands above her head, and clicking her feet):*

Oh, I like that! "Leaping and dancing for the great pleasure it has found in God!" Dance, dance, dance, man, dance! Dance to the Lord, dance to the Lord of the dance! And laughter? Oh, Sir, despite all the world's sorrows and horrors, may the human heart laugh?

LUTHER: The human heart that believes in him is no longer subject to fear. It is invaded by a feeling of delight. It laughs. Yes, verily, it laughs!

ME-T: Oh, Sir, Thomas Hobbes, who lived in the next century after you, said that laughter is nothing else but sudden glory arising from some sudden conception of some eminence in ourselves by comparison with the infirmity of others, *or with our own formerly.*

ME-D *(her face dark again, and her voice tense and harsh):* But not by comparison with the infirmity of others! Oh, no, not that! Don't you see? We always come back to John Bradford again. We come back to the raped body of the ten year old girl. The principle of Grace is wonderful – *for me.* But what of the tragic condition that drives the mind to hell's despair? Am I supposed to feel sudden glory comparing myself to the infirmity of others?

S.K.: Luther, this woman must read your Christmas sermons on that lowly little lovely Epistle of Titus. God's Grace received must be bestowed! Madame, there are *two* principles to Grace. (1) Receiving favors from God. (2) Granting favors to your neighbor. May I add to your inestimable words, Luther, and say – granting favors to the neighbor without feeling that we are doing God a favor!

LUTHER: The two loveliest words Scripture uses of Grace are *chrestotes* (kindness, friendliness) and *philanthropia* (philanthropy, love toward man). Where could Paul have found words that communicated more love and graciousness! They describe Grace not only as forgiving our sins but as God ever present with us, embracing us in his friendship, a friend who is willing to help us – help us to bestow that gift of God, friendliness and love of mankind – upon the neighbor.

S.K.: This woman should read your discourse on "The Freedom of the Christian Man." The two principles of Grace are so clear there: the Word is given to *cleanse* of sin and to *quicken* to good works.

LUTHER: And, mark you, not to live at ease! Good and pious works never make a good and pious man, but a good and pious man does good works. Madame, good works can no more be separated from faith in the Grace of God than light and heat can be separated from a flame. Released from despair, the human heart in gratitude turns to the neighbor, to help him in his despair.

ME-T *(to all the other Me's):* This is what is called the "Therefore" Ethic. Love of the neighbor is the inevitable expression of Grace received.

LUTHER: A better way to say it is, "I live, yet not I." Christ is given to me, and I turn and give Christ to the neighbor. It is audacious but true: *Jeder Christ dem andern ein Christus.* Every Christian a Christ to the other man. *Ich soll mich meinem nächsten als Christus geben.* I am to give myself as Christ to the neighbor.

S.K.: She should read your Preface to the Epistle to the Romans! "Works done against the grain and with reluctance accomplish nothing." Luther, it was you who gave me the two concepts: The Kingdom of the Second Spontaneity and The Double Movement of Infinity. Your description of the zest to live and to love, the spontaneous love to the neighbor, which is created in the forgiven and grateful human heart by the Holy Spirit, guided me to the idea of a *second* spontaneity. . . .

ME-E: . . . on the other side of innocence and ignorance, the little-girl-pink and the little-boy-blue, on the far side of the Land of Tra-la-la, on the far side of the Land of Ish, the cinder in the eye, the bitter black vomit. . . .

80

S.K. *(continuing as if never interrupted):* Your description of the whole process of receiving the Grace of God in Christ and by the power of the Holy Spirit being Christ to the neighbor gave me the idea for the Double Movement of Infinity, that great curve –

ME-E: An elliptical curve! A beautiful elliptical curve! Grace poured out from its Source on me and flowing to the neighbor through me!

ME-T: Now I understand what Pascal meant when he said that genuine morality laughs at Morality.

S.K.: And do you now understand what I meant when I said, "Christ's atonement, his suffering and death, is everything, and transforms the little I do into a jest; whether I reform the whole world or faithfully take care of my job as a hired man, it is one and the same, for Christ's atonement is everything. Grace is the earnestness, my works are only a jest – and so, get going, the more the better, the more spontaneity and verve, the better."

ALL OF MY ME'S: We do! We do!

LUTHER *(laughing heartily):* It seems we are no longer needed. May we go to the rest you pulled us from?

ME-I *(impishly):* Well deserved rest? Merited rest?

LUTHER: Not even this have we deserved! All is Grace, amazing Grace!

*(Whereupon Luther and Kierkegaard promptly disappear and all of my Me's are suddenly transported out of Gilleleie to the seashore and the sand dunes, where they dance and frolic in great sweeping elliptical curves, until Me-D suddenly takes a great running leap and shouts "Christ died for the sins of the whole world!" and leaps to the top of the boulder on which was inscribed:*

> The thing is to find a truth which is true *for me,*
> to find *the idea for which I can live or die.*

*and cries "and for me-e-e-e-e!" She laughs down at the other selves from her high perch.)*

ME-D: I graciously pronounce to you the gracious forgiveness of all your sins!

ME-R *(aghast):* You are not ordained!

ME-D: Grace created the priesthood of all believers!

*(She leaps down among us and dances with us, all of my Me's, in the sand by the sea, until we fall exhausted and into deep and dreamless sleep.)*

decoding

amazing grace

act VII

*Me-R and the fleshly Me are watering the house plants next morning – something we can do quite well in that morning stupor before the other tenants of the mind have awakened and seized the day – when Me-D, my Despair, comes out of her cell wearing zippered black boots and an ankle-long, belted, patch-pocketed black coat. She is carrying – not the week-end bag she usually takes on her short absences – but its large matching pullman bag as well. Her face is white and tragic.*

ME-R: My dear, what is it? Where are you going?

85

ME-D: Don't you see? I can't stay here any more.

ME-R: Mercy me, why not?

*(Just then the other Me's emerge, yawning, from their rooms. They grasp the situation at once and ask the same questions.)*

ME-D: We were all so carried away last night we didn't see the full implications of my leap, my conversion, or whatever it was that happened to me yesterday. I'm beginning to wish it hadn't! Oh, don't you see? It's exodus for me! Adieu and farewell! I have to decamp, evacuate, seek another home!

ALL *(dismayed):* No, no, this is your home!

ME-D *(looking around dejectedly):* It's become a habit to me, and I've become a habit to it. I've become a habit to all of you. In fact, I've become a habit to myself. Don't you see, you sillies? If I'm converted, then I'm not me, Despair, any more. I'm something else. But what? If despair is my habit, my temperament, my addiction, then I can't stay here. If this place is going to be wide-open and surrendered to Grace, every square inch of it, even my private cell, then I can no longer feel at home here. Already I feel strange, estranged, and I'm afraid the cozy, homelike feeling I had will never come again. I want to go away, and yet I don't. And if you are really honest, you will admit that you want me, Despair, to go.

ALL: But we don't! *(But even as they protest they know that they do indeed want that self to go, that melancholy self that sometimes casts the whole place into such a gloom that all the other Me's with the dialectical gift of gab fall silent. And yet they do not want her to go.)*

ME-N: You can't go! You're – why, you're just a natural part of the landscape.

ME-D: I know! *(She bursts into tears, drops her bags, and sits down in the middle of the warm-hued braided wool rug, and the other five sit around her wearing their glummest faces.)*

ME-E *(who has been getting redder and redder in the face and can no longer contain herself):* Well, when's the funeral?

ME-D *(gasping):* You mean me? My funeral?

ME-E *(grimly):* No, your Experience with a capital E. Apparently your Great Experience of yesterday has gone dead, and we might as well bury it!

ME-I *(softly):* We have been hard on each other in the past, but never mean!

ME-E *(savagely):* And let's bury Grace, Gay Grace, along with that Supremely Wonderful Experience! I started the whole thing ranting about John Bradford and rhapsodizing about Gay Grace. Well, I'll end it, too, by inviting you all to the funeral.

ME-D *(jumping to her feet):* Ecstasy, don't you be like me! Don't be as I was before!

ME-E *(also jumps to her feet and faces Despair with blazing fury):* And still are! And still are!

ME-D: No!

ME-E: Yes! Are you a New Creation, a New Woman? Are any of us? Isn't this the same old Big Bust, the same old hangover after a spiritual spree? *(Looks around, talking wildly.)* I thought it would be different this time. I really believed in Gay Grace. I really did! But if Me-D reaches the heights she reached last night and then today slumps, then forever more I will believe the slumps and no longer believe in the heights. Everything passes, everything perishes. I know it now for sure, and believe me, I will never, never let myself get taken in again!

ME-D *(softly):* If I actually have slumped from yesterday's heights and if you, Ecstasy, actually do no longer believe in the heights but only in the slumps, then our despair will be doubled and this house is doomed. Oh, forgive me, Ecstasy! What you just heard me say, what you just witnessed, must be the last gasp of my dying despair. Oh, believe me, all of you, there was an occasion, there was an experience, there was a gift of Grace! If I am not a new creation, something new is creating. What, I am not sure! Everything now depends on how I grasp what was given, how I absorb it. I am temporarily bewildered about what the healed Me will be and how I am to relate to all of you. I do so want to stick around. I like it here! But I need to be needed. If I am going to be the opposite of what I was, I will be Ecstasy, and we already have Ecstasy!

ME-T *(who also has been getting strangely excited and feels another "connection" coming on):* Oh, you muddleheads! If you would bother to think straight, you wouldn't talk yourselves into such dead ends! The opposite of Despair is not Ecstasy! What is despair? Think, now! When you were despondent, wretched, anguished, Despair, you were – what? Utterly hopeless! And the opposite of hopelessness . . . ?

ME-D: The opposite of hopelessness is Hope! *(She plops down on the rug as if she suddenly feels anchored again.)* Hope! Is that my new name? Will I wear it gracefully? Is Grace so great it can change a hopeless Me to a hope-full Me? Is forgiveness power so powerful it can wipe out the habit of despair?

ME-E: Hope! Oh, that's beautiful! Let's make your new name official, and since I was the one who practically plunged us all back into our former condition, let me be the officiating official. *(She snips three perfect red geraniums and tucks them into Me-D's crown of hair.)* By the Grace of God – Father, Son, and Holy Spirit – you are no longer Despair. You are Hope! *(Something of yesterday's elation begins to stir like a rain-drenched fledgling bird drying in the sun but feebly flops again, for Me-H, formerly Despair, is the least elated of all.)*

ME-HOPE (*in a very small voice*): I think I am going to find it very hard at first to be cheerful and hope for the best and make the best of everything and look on the bright side of life and smile all the time and all that –.

ME-E: Oh, come, now! I put red geraniums in your hair, not rose-colored glasses on your nose!

ME-T: Grace does not create Pollyannas! Grace does not make us lose contact with the actuality of evil and ignore the consequences of sin in the world and in our lives! In fact, in your new role as Hope you must not forsake that part of your old role which was most salutary to every one of us several selves.

As Despair you constantly reminded us of the tragic human condition which drove your mind to hell's despair, and as Hope you must continue to do so – but in *hope,* without plunging into that old nightmare. I needed you, and I will continue to need you. My temptation as a pseudo-theologian is the temptation of every theologian – to use terms like Grace, new birth, justification, atonement, as if they were scientific terms. Our temptation is to spend so much time talking about them that we begin to imagine that we have had or are having the experience of them. We study concepts so hard to learn how to live that we never live.

As Despair you reminded me always how far I was from being what I theologized about. You must continue to do so! Never let me forget how this female who is always talking about the Grace of God needs that Grace!

ME-R: I'm a conservative, traditionalist Christian, as you all know – and continually remind me! Always have been, always will be – and I will always need you to save me from becoming a Christian stereotype, a spiritual egotist. By constantly reminding me of the desperate plight of mankind, the scandal of man's injustice to man, you kept me from the traditional habits of mind of most traditionalists and conservatives – self-righteousness coupled with indifference to the pain and suffering of mankind. I need you to puncture the feelings of worthiness I get from keeping the traditions and following the rites and rituals – so that I will know my need of Grace, so that my adoration of God and my love for the neighbor will not dry up.

ME-E *(soberly):* I hated you, Despair, for I always wanted to ascend, and you always made me descend. To me life was beauty, and you made life a duty. I suppose I'm the perennial adolescent in this combination – impatiently longing for another time, another condition, the pure moment. I made Christianity into a superlativity and would have ended in a kind of mysticism if it had not been for you. You kept bringing me back out of my bliss to the wretchedness of earth. You kept putting me in the neighbor's shoes so that all my personal feeling-experiences faded into nothingness, and I became ashamed of them.

Oh, keep doing so! As Hope, keep on showing me that neighbor in front of my nose! Make me see that his life is no less living than my life! Make me realize that pain in him and joy in him and grief in him and love in him are just as much pain and joy and grief and love in *him,* whatever his race and color or age or sex, as they are in *me.* Make him as much a self to me as I am to myself!

Make me *know* my neighbor, and then I will know how I have failed in my duty to him. Then I will know the sin and selfishness of my private enjoyment of the gifts of God. Then I will know how rightly to use the Grace of God.

ME-I: Steel yourselves, darlings! I've been the one who has always blurted and blabbed off the top of our head, but you have never heard from me what you are going to hear now. I have a feeling I will need you more in the future, Hope, but let me say here and now that as Despair you served me well! By honestly showing me the ultimate nullity and nothingness of every human attempt to create a second Eden, you saved me from that sin of optimism which conceives of the progressive elimination of sin and evil. In my youth I played the game of Revolt Against Everything. Remember, the high school annual called me an iconoclast! Well, believe it or not, now I'm just an iconoclast gone to seed. I'm tired and disillusioned. That surprises you, doesn't it? You all think me flip and funny. I'm willing to wager that inside of every wisecracking, bantering wag there's a defeated idealist trying to hide behind a pun. I need you, Hope, for all my hopes died with all my ideals!

ME-N: And me? Shy, quiet little old me? I was a pagan, Despair – I mean Hope – and you kept me conscious of it. I didn't want that self-knowledge! I loved the landscape and hated the humanscape. I kept fuming at men for their inability to see with what Dylan Thomas called his "five and country senses," and you kept reminding me that I was too ignorant and too selfish to help carry the burden of evil in this world.

I loathed men for their defilement and pollution of nature, and you kept reminding me of my own defilement and pollution.

My eyes were tuned to streams and mountains, and you kept thrusting human misery in between and put me out of tune with my self. Oh, I hated you! All the time that I needed you I hated you!
*(All the Me's look unbearably down in the mouth. Ecstasy, shorn of glory, resembles a shorn and shaven French poodle.)*

ME-HOPE *(with a sudden peal of laughter):* Oh, a comet just streaked into my mind! You dopes! You sillies! It wasn't I who drove you to self-knowledge, guilt, and shame. It was the Spirit! I didn't remind you. It was the Spirit!

I did not hold you up against Christ. It was the Spirit! I didn't shove the neighbor under your nose. It was the Spirit!

What was I? I was your blush, your humbled pride. I was your guilt, your shame. I was your despair, your hopelessness. I was your choosing not to be a self, one united self related to God, related to the neighbor. I was your despair, your sickness unto death.

When I ran and leaped upon the rock, I was your confession of your need of Grace. I was your gratitude for Grace. I was your commitment to the God of Grace. I was your pledge to love the neighbor.

You may call me Hope from now on, but Christ alone is our hope. And it is Spirit who binds us changeful children to the Unchanging Love. I can do nothing, only be the expression of your hope in him, even as I have been the expression of your hopelessness. But call me Hope – oh, do! I love my new name!

ME-T: I'm not sure that you haven't turned into *me!* That was the most theologically beautiful thing I have heard for a long time, Hope. But your name fits you perfectly. Just as Despair expressed our misrelation to God and to each other, expressed our flight away from the Eternal, so the name Hope expresses our gift of Grace and our relationship to God and our new relationship to each other. For it *is* new! I feel its newness. As Despair you did not make us a weaker I, you only expressed our weakness. As Hope you do not make us a stronger I, you express the Grace-faith relation which holds us all to God and together and makes us a healed I and therefore a stronger I.

ME-IMP: In other words, as Despair you helped bring us into the right relationship to the Divine Equation, and we have a lot to thank you for.

ME-H: Not me, not me! The Spirit! It was the Spirit!

ME-I *(chanting):*

Our fractions had no togetherness.
They never voted unanimous.
Since they were not homogenous,
Our fractioned selves were disharmonious.

And you were our despair over that, and because of you, our despair, we were brought face to face with Christ on the cross and found wholeness.

In him alone
In him atoned
Our variables found their constant
Our divided selves at-one-ment.

ME-T: That is the most theological bad poetry you have ever made up. I am delighted by the perspicacity you are all suddenly showing. Verily, verily, there is hope for us!

ME-N *(stretches to her tallest, suddenly collapses gracefully to a comfortable squat):* You know, sisters dear, for the first time in my life I feel legitimate! I've sometimes felt like the unbaptized pagan in the Congregation of the Select Elect. In this baptism of the Spirit I am legitimized! Without me you would be unaware of all the small delights that are God's daily gift in his creation. Without me you would not see that the hyacinths are pushing through the ground, would not rejoice in the onions sprouting in the shopping bag, struggling against all odds for life and light.

ME-R: And even Ye Olde Conventionalist Me can hold her head up in our relationship in the Spirit! Without me you would not have much continuity in your lives. I keep you in the Word and the sacraments and the liturgy and the church. I am not so obsolete after all!

ME-I: Hear ye! Hear ye! I feel the faint stirrings of my old radical self, but blessed by the Spirit! I shall call you – not to rebellion, but to radical discipleship. Watch out, we may all as one find ourselves in conflict with many of the customs, attitudes, and systems of the day!

ME-E: And I shall keep watch on *you*, so that you never forget love – the love that embraced and embraces us in Grace and fills us full to spilling over. What a wonderful thought it is! No one can walk with a full cup without spilling.

ME-R: Peter said it in more traditional language – at least, it has become traditional!

> "Come to him, to that living stone, rejected by men but in God's sight chosen and precious; and like living stones be yourselves built into a spiritual house, to be a holy priesthood, to offer spiritual sacrifices acceptable to God through Jesus Christ."

ME-H *(utterly amazed):* So the gift was not just to me, and we are all a new creation! And God used even my despairing self to draw us to him and to each other. He made Grace out of my despair. Amazing Grace! And now I am no longer Despair but Hope. We have become a self, and I am at home here and may stay forever!

ME-I: Let's celebrate! Have an Open House! Invite everybody! Have a Grace-In Laugh-In!

94

ME-H *(shyly):* **Do** you mind? I feel so grateful I think I'd rather pray today –
and tomorrow we can celebrate.

*(Which they do all the time the fleshly Me, strangely motivated, cleans house all day long. For my several selves discover that with their new self and in the latitude and freedom of Grace they can pray while I wield a broom, run the vacuum cleaner, empty ash trays of old cigar butts, clean dead ashes out of the fireplace. Me-E discovers that she can say grace for new leaves on the house plants as I pluck off the dead ones. Me-N discovers that she can ask forgiveness of both God and the spiders when she sweeps down cobwebs. Me-R finds herself praying for the people who call to chat on the phone, instead of rebelling at the interruption in her routine. She later confides that she has learned the difference between devotion and devotions and prefers the former by far. And when I kneel to build a fresh fire in the fireplace, Me-E suddenly reminds me of an old poem):*

THE SACRAMENT OF FIRE

BY JOHN OXENHAM

Kneel always when you light a fire!
Kneel reverently, and thankful be
For God's unfailing charity;
And on the ascending flame inspire
A little prayer, that shall upbear
The incense of your thankfulness
For this sweet grace
Of warmth and light;
For here again is sacrifice
For your delight.

95

Within the wood,
That lived a joyous life
Through sunny days and rainy days
And winter storms and strife –
Within the peat
That drank the sweet,
The moorland sweet
Of bracken, whin, and sweet bell-heather,
And knew the joy of gold gorse feather
Flaming like love in wintriest weather,

While snug below, in sun and snow,
It heard the beat of the padding feet
Of foal and dam, and ewe and lamb,
And the stamp of old bell-wether;–
Within the coal,
Where forests lie entombed,
Oak, elm, and chestnut, beech, and red pine bole;–
God shrined his sunshine and enwombed
For you these stores of light and heat,
Your life-joys to complete.
These all have died that you might live;
Yours now the high prerogative
To loose their long captivities,
And through these new activities
A wiser life to give.

Kneel always when you light a fire!
Kneel reverently,
And grateful be
For God's unfailing charity!

open house
in dialectical hall
act VIII

*Despite the new harmony among my several selves, decorating for Open House Dialectical Hall almost becomes a riot. Me-R is determined to have great wreaths and garlands of pink double Gibson roses, Me-N would agree to roses only if they are wild. Me-E goes into ecstasies over a seed and nursery catalog and wants to fill the Hall with everything she sees pictured – huge frilly double petunias, hanging baskets of Mexican Beauty geraniums, skyscraper glads, exotic cannas, giant dahlias, purple wisteria. Me-T raises her voice for the lowly vegetable, claiming that there is nothing more beautiful than climbing tomatoes and pole beans, bright golden pumpkins, blazing red peppers, and hubbard squash. But Me-H wistfully suggests that they adorn the hall with the scenes and scents of spring, the season of hope and newness in God's creation, the symbol of resurrection and eternal hope for the human spirit. To that suggestion there is not one dissenting voice, and suddenly Dialectical Hall is full of the odors, tastes, touches, smells, sights, and sounds of April.*

ME-E *(whispering):* I thought we should have Bach and Vivaldi on the stereo for background music, but what better music is there than spring peepers?

ME-T: And I thought we should have incense, but what incense is more fragrant of adoring love than the scent of the hyacinths?

*(Strangely enough, Dialectical Hall has become extraordinarily spacious – indeed, large enough for trees that thrust out budding branches, seeming to invite . . .)*

ME-H: Banners!

*(And they run here and there hanging bright banners until every tree is a prolific banner-bearing tree. It is not difficult to tell which Me has hung what where. They read each other's Gracewords with delight.*

L ᴬ U ᴳ H
at all you
*t r e m b l e d*
at before.

WILLIAM COWPER

GRACE
gives a
greater
EDEN
than the
one you *lost.*

wHo'S aFrAid oF
OrIgiNaL sIn?

102

I believe in forGIVEness POWER!

For my
*STRENGTH*
is made
perfect
*in weakness!*

ST. PAUL

C
L
I
N
G
TO GRACE
*AND LIVE IT*
R
A
D
I
C
A
L
L
Y

DAMN gravitates  BLESS levitates

Forgiveness o p e n s man to man

*The*
*one*
*enemy*
*you*
*cannot*
*conquer*
*BY YOURSELF*
*IS YOURSELF*
*You*
*need*
*grace!*

JESUS CHRIST
OUR HOPE OUR JOY
ST. PAUL

for adOration
all the
paths of grace
are Open.

CHRISTOPHER SMART

FORGIVENESS OPENS
REACHES TO OTHERS

who can neglect
SO GREAT
a salvation  ?

EPISTLE TO THE HEBREWS

COME BOLDLY TO THE   THRONE

OF GRACE

grace  A  *leaves*
heals  N  *no*
hurts  D  *scars*

GRACE is to be continually *reborn*
and we cannot be *reborn*
enough

GRACE
the bare

GOODNESS

of God

MARTIN LUTHER

THE DEATH
OF DEATH
AT LAST
! ! ! ! !

HOSEA

NOT by      BUT by the
    fleshly          grace
    wisdom         of God   ST. PAUL

*An OUNCE*
*of God's Grace*
*is worth a TON*
*of moralizing*

My grace is
  *sufficient* for you

Grace is not
It is the gift ST. PAUL your doing.
of God.

God resists
the PROUD
and to
the humble
he gives grace
ST. PETER

Grace and truth came by Jesus Christ. ST. JOHN

The law was given by Moses

I would rather be
  mad
  with
  grace
than sane
  with
  a
  system
  •

GRACE
  IN
GROW
GLOW
  IN
  GRACE

BIG
NO WIGS IN
  GRACE—
  ONLY CLOWNS I

ME-R *(dubiously):* Dialectical Hall is beginning to look like a stage for a Laugh-In.

ME-E: That's what we are having – a Grace-In Laugh-In. Is everybody ready? Shall we open the doors?

ME-N: What if nobody comes?

ME-H: Of course the Friends of Grace will come! But remember, don't anybody think anybody! Let's make it a real *Happening!* Ready? O.K. Open the doors!

ME-I *(stifling a squeal):* I wonder who will be first?

*(For one blank moment there is nobody. A whippoorwill sings on a distant brain ridge, making the hall seem lonely and isolated. They do not see him at first, for they are watching the doors, and he does not come through any door. He is just suddenly there, dressed in tights and full-sleeved blouse iridescent with all the colors of the rainbow. He dances lightly into their midst, carrying with ease and grace on upraised arms and outstretched palms – not his former somber burden, but a squirming portly burden in clerical black.)*

ME-H *(radiant):* It is you! O Bliss, O Joy! You came back. We know your secret now. It is Grace, Gay Grace, Amazing Grace!

*(His face is kindled and enkindling, a ravishing blend of rapture and mirth. The halo of something miraculous envelops him and them and fills the room, until the banners no longer express what ought to be but is. He pirouettes nimbly on his toes and then fluently sets his burden on its two stout feet. Me-E stares at the stranger.)*

ME-E *(gasping):* John Bradford!

BRADFORD *(straightening his frock coat):* My gracious Lady, I know not where

I am or why I came, or who the harlequin is who brought me, but God grace your soul, I am at your service.

ME-E: Did you actually ever say: "There but for the grace of God goes John Bradford?"

BRADFORD: Aye, Madame, that I did – before I knew that I would go their way – not hang, but burn.

ME-E: They burned you? You died a martyr's death?

BRADFORD: Aye, Madame I died in flame. Though chaplain to King Edward VI, son of Henry VIII and Jane Seymour, I was not spared.

ME-E *(urgently):* Do you feel that Grace took away its gracious hand?

BRADFORD *(surprised):* Nay, prithee, Woman, Grace was with me all the more! Grace helped me defy their every attempt to make me yield. Grace took my soul from my scorched body to the throne of Grace – and truly, it did not even reek of flame.

ME-E *(bowing her head humbly):* Forgive me! I did not know, I did not understand. I did you wrong!

BRADFORD: I know not of what you speak, Gentle Woman, but no matter, we are heartily well met. This is a fair and festive edifice, and I have most cause to be glad to be here.

ME-T: Welcome to our Open House for Grace, John Bradford, and welcome to you, too, Mr. Tumbler, Mr. Juggler, or whoever you are. *(Me-T's eyes widen as the Tumbler whirls toward the door, leaps high, and somersaults without moving from the spot in the face of three new arrivals. John Bradford makes a sweeping 16th century bow that almost tumbles him. My Me's realize that these are prestigious guests but fail to recognize them.)*

ALL OF MY ME'S *(in a stage whisper):* Who are they?

BRADFORD: St. John, St. Paul, and St. Augustine!

ALL OF MY ME's *(in a veritable tizzy):* We never expected saints!

ME-R *(gushing with cordiality):* Ah, we are graced indeed to have St. John, the Ambassador of God's love, St. Paul, the Ambassador of God's Grace and the greatest apostle of them all, and St. Augustine, the greatest of the Latin Fathers at our Open House for Grace!

PAUL *(sharply):* I am the *least* of the apostles, unfit to be called an apostle because I persecuted the church of God. By the Grace of God I am what I am, and his Grace toward me was not in vain. On the contrary, I worked harder than any of them, though it was not I, but the Grace of God which was in me.

JOHN: And from his fulness we have all received, Grace upon Grace!

AUGUSTINE: I came late to love my God. I sought Truth in all the books of the Platonists, but I could not abandon my concupiscence, I did not find the Word that healed, I did not learn to rejoice in grace and forgiveness until I read Holy Scripture. Then these truths did wonderfully sink into my bowels, especially when I read this least of his apostles *(pointing to Paul).* I did not forsake my scorching bed of unchastity until my eyes fell upon this least one's words:

> "Not in rioting and drunkenness,
> not in chambering and wantonness,
> not in strife and envying;
> but put ye on the Lord Jesus Christ,
> and make no provision for the flesh."

And when I read further it said, "Him that is weak in the faith, receive . . .," and God took my weakness and filled it with his Grace.

ME-H *(whispers to herself):* What are saints but weak things filled with Grace!

*(But yet another saint arrives, and never was there more fanfare than that which heralds the arirval of this slight man wearing something resembling a too-big brown burlap potato sack with a rope tied around his middle. Curled around his neck and affectionately nibbling his right ear is our pet raccoon! We recognize this one at once – St. Francis. At his heels are all our pets, noisily romping and capering as if the cats are drunk on catnip and the dogs on – what? Do dogs get drunk on dogma?*

*On the heels of the St. Francis and the pets come such an assortment of guests as anyone could ever hope to see at any Open House ever. They arrive from every age, but they are ageless. They have this agelessness in common, for – to paraphrase one of those present, Sir Thomas Browne – they do not date their Grace and mercy from God from the date of their birth, but they looked beyond the world and before the era of Adam.*

*Another thing they have in common is that all the pain and grief they ever knew in time is as if it had never been, for they have not made their heads repositories of life's damages and disappointments, but of God's Grace.*

*But perhaps the most striking characteristic the guests that stream into our Open House have in common is gratitude, gratitude for Grace! There are those who say that Children of Grace are God's pampered people and that the Kingdom of Grace is an illusory Kingdom of All the Wished-Fors, a Kingdom of Four-Leaf Clovers, but these guests are praising people whose only wish is to glorify God for his Grace. Indeed, they even glorify the thorns and arrows in their flesh! Me-I listens eagerly to Sebastian (martyred in 288) and Bonhoeffer (martyred in World War II) and Father Dan Berrigan (imprisoned in 1970) talking about the joyous, audacious freedom in the teeth of the law that comes to one who has been "sucked clean of the old antibiotic slaveries and fears, the nightmarish sense of being frozen in his place, frozen in moral gesture, incapable of love or comparison or purity."*

*Me-T overhears Bobby Burns – probably attracted by the festive sounds and looking for rollicking fun – express his amazement to Bob Russ, who rolls up in his wheelchair just before the doors have to be closed because no brain on earth can contain any more people, that this motley assemblage in no way resembles "those sighin', cantin', grace-proud faces with three-mile prayers and half-mile graces" that he had known when he lived in time. Bob, who still lives in time, shouts so loudly with laughter that Luther comes over, looms over his flawed and faulted body with his own Falstaffian bulk and wants to know what the joke is, which leads to a lively dialog between Bob and Luther on the Apollonian and Dionysian poles of Grace. Bobbie Burns walks away shaking his head.*

*There are women at our Open House, too, and despite the presence of several notorious female-repressionists, they do not keep silent. Praise flows from them as freely as from the men. Mary and Mary Magdalene walk about with winsome grace magnifying their Lord. When Luther the theologian is not holding forth on the "bare goodness of God," Luther the proud husband is introducing "Katie my rib" to everyone.*

*Another proud husband and wife wandering about hand in hand and extolling Grace are Elizabeth Barret Browning and Robert. Evelyn Underhill, Dorothy Day, and Christina Rossetti are present, too, their faces proving what Christina once wrote: "A merry heart is a continual feast."*

*Suddenly in the eastern end of Dialectical Hall there shines a rainbow arch of light, one end resting on the astonished faces of the guests clustered there and the other in some invisible place outside of my brain, outside of* time. *"Bridge of the Holy Spirit," "Girdle of God," the rainbow is called in some languages, and truly this one seems to be a holy effulgence. The lively talk dwindles away to a hushed silence. Even the pets are still. The guests enveloped with the radiance move back, and a bare stage rises before their eyes. Into the violet center of the arch springs the Tumbler and does his tumbling, juggling act, gliding across the stage through violet, indigo, blue, green, yellow, orange, and red – and back again to violet. When he leaps back among us again, no one claps, not one, not even Bobbie Burns, but all stand rapt, especially Bobbie Burns!*

*The violet center of the stage is immediately taken by a man who never wore a mask in time, a man who T. S. Eliot said "was naked, and saw man naked, and from the center of his own crystal." William Blake stands in the light as if he is accustomed to standing in visions and speaks – believe me, it is not reciting! – his thoughts in utterly simple words, but nobody is fooled by their simpleness.)*

WILLIAM BLAKE:

> I saw a chapel all of gold
> That none did dare to enter in,
> And many weeping stood without,
> Weeping, mourning, worshipping.
>
> I saw a serpent rise between
> The white pillars of the door,
> And he forc'd and forc'd;
> Down the golden hinges tore.

And along the pavement sweet,
Set with pearls and rubies bright,
All his shining length he drew,
Till upon the altar white

Vomiting his poison out
On the bread and on the wine.
So I turn'd into a sty
And laid me down among the swine.

ME-I:  Oh, the party-pooper! The party-pooper! He's spoiling everything!
ME-T *(hissing):* Be quiet, you ninny! Wait and listen!

WILLIAM BLAKE:

Jesus was sitting in Moses' chair,
They brought the trembling woman there.
Moses commands she be stoned to death.
What was the sound of Jesus' breath?
He laid his hand on Moses' law;
The ancient Heaven, in silent awe,
Writ wider curses from pole to pole,
All away began to roll.

*(He pauses for a moment, and we wait in silence.)*

WILLIAM BLAKE:

And throughout all Eternity
I forgive you, you forgive me.
As our dear Redeemer said:
"This the Wine, and this the Bread."

*(And then with a lilting voice he breaks into his "Laughing Song".)*

WILLIAM BLAKE:

> When the green woods laugh with the voice of joy,
> And the dimpling stream runs laughing by;
> When the air does laugh with our merry wit,
> And the green hill laughs with the noise of it;
> When the meadow laughs with lively green,
> And the grasshopper laughs in the merry scene,
> When Mary and Susan and Emily
> With their sweet round mouths sing "Ha, ha, he!"
> When the painted birds laugh in the shade,
> When our table with cherries and nuts is spread,
> Come live, and be merry, and join with me,
> To sing the sweet chorus of "Ha, ha, he!"

ME-T: Don't you see? It's the proper sequence! It's the path of Grace! From grief to laughter.

ME-H: But not the Double Movement of Infinity! He leaves out the movement of Grace to the neighbor.

ME-T: Ah, but he did not. Read *all* his poetry, look at his paintings, and you will see all those for whom "the sun does never shine and their fields are bleak and bare, and their ways are filled with thorns."

*(As if to speak the yet unspoken, St. Augustine comes onto the stage and peers intently down at all the upraised faces.)*

ST. AUGUSTINE: Do you want to know if God is there? When you turn to him, have you the interest of humanity in your heart? When you try to approach God, do you bring with you human kind and all its cares? Do you bring

113

with you those whom he gave you to love? If mankind is present in your tenderness and love, then God is there.

ME-I: Ach, du lieber Augustine! Oh, you precious man! What a way to put it! *(Christina Rossetti puts it into poetry for us. She stands in the lavender light, frail and marked by suffering, with eyes luminous with joy, and quietly gives us her gift of Grace, "Because He First Loved Us.")*

> I was hungry, and you fed me;
> You gave me drink to slake my thirst.
> O Lord, what love gift can I offer you,
> who loved me first?
>
> Feed my hungry brothers for my sake;
> Give them drink, for love of them and me.
> Love them as I loved you, when bread I broke
> In pure love of thee.
>
> Yes, Lord, I will serve them by your grace;
> Love you, seek you, in them; wait and pray.
> Yet would I love yourself, Lord, face to face,
> Heart to heart, one day.

ME-E: Perfect! Perfect! The sequence of Grace is perfect! And then the sequel – the hope of meeting him face to face. From grief to laughter to glory. Oh, Christina, I love you!

*(And now John Bunyan, "who lay so long at Sinai," yet lived to write* Pilgrim's Progress *and* Grace Abounding to the Chief of Sinners, *bounds on-*

*stage and in full, powerful voice, accustomed to preaching the Gospel of Grace to crowds of peasants, tells the story of his conversion.)*

JOHN BUNYAN: I heard one preach a sermon upon these words in the Song of Solomon, "Behold thou art fair, my Love." The words began thus to kindle in my Spirit. "Thou art my Love, Thou art my Love," twenty times together; and still as they ran thus in my mind they waxed stronger and warmer and began to make me look up – then I began to give place to the Word, which with power did over and over make this joyful sound within my soul, *Thou art my Love, Thou art my Love;* and nothing shall separate *me from my love;* and with that Romans 8:39 came into my mind. Now was my heart full of comfort and hope, and now I could believe that my sins would be forgiven; yea, I was now so taken with the love and mercy of God, that I remember I could not tell how to contain it 'till I got home; I thought I could have spoke of his Love and his mercy to all, even to the very crows that sat upon the plowed land.

ME-I *(to Me-T):* What is Romans 8:39?

*(As if to answer her question, the swarthy Paul with the burning eyes appears on the stage.)*

PAUL: Grace to you and peace from God our Father and the Lord Jesus Christ! We are now more than conquerors through him who loved us. For I am sure that neither death, nor life, nor angels, nor principalities, nor things present, nor things to come, nor powers, nor height, nor depth, nor anything else in all creation, will be able to separate us from the love of God in Christ Jesus our Lord.

*(St. Paul has no sooner left the stage when a man who looks more like a sot than a saint gets through the red rainbow light as far as the orange before Me-R grabs him.)*

ME-R: *Stop!* You can't be here!

SAUL KANE: Madame, I *am* here! I am Saul Kane, whom Miss Bourne, the Quaker woman who goes around "to all the pubs in the place to bring the drunkards' souls to grace" converted and brought from darkness into light.

ME-R: But you are fictitious, not real! You are a character in John Masefield's "The Everlasting Mercy."

SAUL KANE: Is this room a mind?

ME-R: It is.

SAUL KANE: In the room of the mind the imagined is as real as the actual.

ME-R: But you are a drunkard!

SAUL KANE: *Was,* Madame! And is this not an Open House for Grace? Is Grace not spacious enough for a born-again drunkard?

AUGUSTINE *(imperiously):* Let him speak, Madame! I, whom you called the greatest of the Latin Fathers of the church, am a converted profligate. I, whom you call saint, was addicted to the sins of unchastity. It was a violent habit, and when the battle between Lust and Continence grew strong, I prayed: Lord, make me chaste – *but not yet!* Would you hear more of it, Madame?

*(Me-R grows pale and steps back. Saul Kane stands in the forgiving light and tells his story.)*

> I did not think, I did not strive,
> The deep peace burnt my me alive;
> The bolted door had broken in,
> I knew that I had done with sin.
> I knew that Christ had given me birth
> To brother all the souls on earth,

And every bird and every beast
Should share the crumbs broke at the feast.

*(The story ascends until it becomes a hymn to Grace, lacking only the musical notes. The story-teller is obviously drunk – not with wine but Grace.)*

O ploughman of the sinner's soul
O Jesus, drive the coulter deep
To plough my living man from sleep.
O Christ, who drives the furrow straight,
O Christ, the plough, O Christ, the laughter
Of holy white birds flying after,
Lo, all my heart's field red and torn,
And thou wilt bring the young green corn,
The young green corn divinely springing,
The young green corn forever singing;
And when the field is fresh and fair
Thy blessèd feet shall glitter there,
And we will walk the weeded field,
And tell the golden harvest's yield,
The corn that makes the holy bread
By which the soul of man is fed,
The holy bread, the food unpriced,
Thy everlasting mercy, Christ.

*(The sot turned saint ends his story with these unblemished immaculate lines.)*

117

O lovely lily clean,
O lily spring green,
O lily bursting white,
Dear lily of delight,
Spring in my heart again
That I may flower to men.

*(Me-R, to her everlasting credit, takes Saul Kane's hands in hers and whispers through tears.)*
ME-R: Forgive me!
*(Luther is filled with the same Grace Abounding as John Bunyan and St. Paul and Saul Kane but cannot encase it in words only. Being Martin Luther, he has to make a Homeric hymn of it. He grabs his lute from a linden tree, strides onstage, and sings his odyssey from "Satan's chains" to Grace and victory in a ten stanza hymn.)*

MARTIN LUTHER:

Dear Christians, one and all, rejoice,
With exultation springing,
And, with united heart and voice
And holy rapture singing,
Proclaim the wonders God hath done,
How his right arm the victory won;
Right dearly it hath cost him.

*(Who could resist such an invitation?)*
ME-E: Shall we, oh, shall we?
ME-N: Shall we what?

ME-E: Sing "Amazing Grace" for them?

ME-R: You know we can't sing.

ME-H: In the imagination and in the Hall of Grace an untaught fiddler can play a Paganini and a sparrow sing like a nightingale.

*(And so we do, yes we do, indeed, we six climb onto the stage and sing "Amazing Grace"!)*

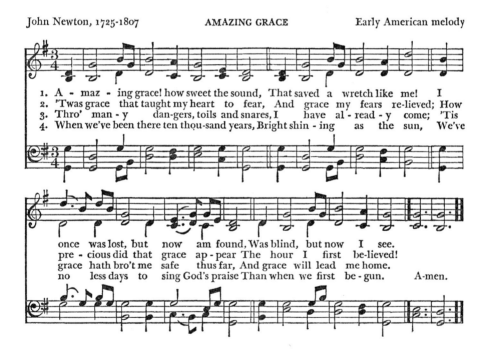

John Newton, 1725-1807      **AMAZING GRACE**      Early American melody

1. A - maz - ing grace! how sweet the sound, That saved a wretch like me! I
2. 'Twas grace that taught my heart to fear, And grace my fears re-lieved; How
3. Thro' man - y dan-gers, toils and snares, I have al - read - y come; 'Tis
4. When we've been there ten thou-sand years, Bright shin - ing as the sun, We've

once was lost, but now am found, Was blind, but now I see.
pre - cious did that grace ap - pear The hour I first be-lieved!
grace hath bro't me safe thus far, And grace will lead me home.
no less days to sing God's praise Than when we first be - gun. A-men.

*(And nobody laughs! In fact, they join us on the last stanza, and we who are yet in time are not so sure of it! Bliss and beatitude, however, are impossible to sustain in mortal beings, indeed, unbearable beyond the fourth or fifth exclamation points. Thank God, Bob Russ senses it first.)*

BOB RUSS: Party's over!

*(He spins his wheel chair toward the door, although he festoons his exit with loops and circles, and instead of going out the door when he reaches it the first time, wheels around the Great Hall. Suddenly the air is filled with the music of a Bach fugue. All the guests fall in step behind the wheel chair and, miraculously, a gayly illuminated poster sprouts in every guest's hands. The exit becomes a Grand Recessional. Bob's sign contains his own lines.)*

> Come down, O Lord,
> Lift up our hearts.
> Dance with us here
> > in time!

*(St. Paul blossoms out with a Freedom Poster.)*

> For freedom Christ has set us free; stand fast therefore, and do not submit again to a yoke of slavery!

*(Søren Kierkegaard carries a poster in each hand.)*

> The more conception of God, the more Self,
> The more Self, the more conception of God.

> The more tuned to God,
> The more tuned to the neighbor.

*(Francis Thompson traipses after him with –)*

To have Grace in the soul is to live in a nutshell and count yourself king of infinite space.

THOMAS MERTON: Seek the living God, not psychological comfort.

JOHN DONNE: Any man's death diminishes *me* because I am involved in mankind; And therefore never send to know for whom the bell tolls; it tolls for *thee*.

WILLIAM BLAKE: A Robin Redbreast in a cage
Puts all heaven in a rage.

JOHN BUNYAN: A man there was, tho' some did count him mad, The more he cast away, the more he had.

BONHOEFFER: Only now are we beginning to discover the meaning of free responsibility. It depends upon a God who demands bold action as the free response of faith, and who promises forgiveness and consolation to the man who becomes a sinner in the process.

*(An anonymous guest none of us recognizes carries a poster that says:)*

Let those love now, who never loved before.
Let those who always loved, now love the more.

*(As each Open House guest reaches the door the second time, he turns to us, bows, smiles, and goes out. Luther and his Katie are the last to disappear, but before they go Luther hands Katie his poster and lifts his hands in benediction. Katie holds the beautifully illuminated message high.)*

> But the bare goodness of God is what ought rather to be preached and known above all else, and we ought to learn, that, even as God saves us out of pure goodness, without any merit or works, so we in turn should do the works without reward of self-seeking, for the sake of the bare goodness of God!

LUTHER: The Grace of the Lord Jesus Christ be with your spirit!

*(They are gone, all the guests to our Grace-In Open House are gone. We look at each other.)*

ME-R: The Juggler? What happened to him? I didn't see him go out in the Recessional. John Bradford went out, but not the Juggler.

ME-E: I think that he will always be present. He will never leave us.

ME-H: I hope and pray that he will never leave us.

ME-T *(firmly):* Hope, my dear, we have untangled so many jumbled ideas — don't go creating more! Pray that *we* do not absent *ourselves,* for he does not! Never!